Maxims of Equity

MAXIMS OF EQUITY

A Juridical Critique of the Ethics of Chancery Law

MICHAEL LEVENSTEIN

Algora Publishing
New York

Library of Congress Cataloging-in-Publication Data —

Levenstein, Michael David, author.
    Maxims of equity: A Juridical Critique of the Ethics of Chancery Law /
Michael David Levenstein.
        pages cm
    Includes bibliographical references and index.
        ISBN 978-1-62894-051-0 (soft cover: alk. paper) — ISBN 978-1-62894-052-7
(hard cover: alk. paper) — ISBN 978-1-62894-053-4 (ebook) 1. Equity—Great
Britain. 2. Equity—Great Britain—Philosophy. I. Title.
    KD674.L48 2014
    174'.3—dc23
                2013050023

Printed in the United States

for my Parents—
Equity's Darlings

TABLE OF CONTENTS

PROLEGOMENON: TWO DOMINIONS OF VIRTUE

OFTEN IS IT SAID that law and morality, however related, are distinct characters unto themselves, twins separated at birth. Brethren which, upon maturity, separately seek the inculcation of civic and ethical excellence to citizen and moral agent alike. Why this is so, and more pressingly, whether it should be, shall be the focus of our opening remarks. It has become all too fashionable to suffer amnesia as regards the import of much esoteric study, hubristically viewing its pursuit to yield an incontrovertible good in itself, and, whilst the law is perhaps further removed from this fault than other disciplines, it nevertheless behooves us to identify the principled and practical foundations (that is, if they are not one and the same) for the necessity of laws in our society. The purpose of this essay is a preliminary exposition of an independent moral code and the extent to which its edicts are applied in various guises across multiple areas of English law. The moral framework presented is designed to include the most prominent values upheld in contemporary civil and political society, albeit one which, like any axiology, is destined to prove controversial in certain quarters. The principal rationale for its inclusion, however, is to illustrate the interrelationship between the enforcement of morals generally, and the inevitable fissures which divide ethics from the legal order. In so doing, we must first begin with a generic philosophical examination of value, proceed to its translation within the legal sphere, and culminate with an enquiry as regards what grounds separate the two fields.

Of Moral Clarity

For millennia, thinkers of all allegiances have engaged in an interminable intellectual imbroglio as regards the Good and how best to achieve the moral clarity it promises to afford. Nowhere has the promise of the Good been sharper than as regards the conception of the legal order—the relationship between State and citizen which affords the latter his rights and duties. For Hobbes, the primal *bellum omnium contra omnes* is pacified through social cooperation only under the iron fist of authoritarianism; for Locke, even in the state of Nature the promise of obedience to moral law is found, but one ever susceptible to the partiality absent from administrative justice. In turn, society becomes justified as the institutionalization writ large of objective morality, whose ultimate function is to magnify benefit to the individual from a brutal free-for-all to a cohesive social unit in which his security is far better ensured.

At the forefront of the philosophical dispute, three schools of thought in particular—virtue ethics, deontology and consequentialism (namely in the guise of utilitarianism)—have captured scholars' imaginations as viable candidates for a grand unified theory of ethics, and by extension, the sociopolitical order. Rather than entertaining so fanciful an ambition in this brief introduction, an altogether alternative conception is posed whose aim is to reconcile these competing frameworks into one which subsumes elements of each, whilst demonstrating that none holds a monopoly on moral truth and that all contribute to the development and purposes of legislative change. Ultimately, this approach unfolds to support the supremacy of consequentialist logic, and a revised utilitarianism which is able to combine the rationalized universality of deontological principle with the focus of individual character as espoused by Aristotelian virtue ethics. The hybridized species of utilitarianism which results uniquely combines a qualitative hierarchy of pleasure with the demands of practical justice to forge a dynamic moral theory which is not only prescriptive, but accurately describes essential components of contemporary jurisprudential thinking.

Philosophy is a discipline distinct from legal science precisely because of its reliance upon reason alone—as opposed to considerations of social practicability—as the lowest common denominator by which propositions may be tested for their veracity via discourse. Accordingly, the ethical framework advanced shall be governed by a materialistic, atheistic metaphysics, one in whose only refuge for moral, let alone any legal, enlightenment is the preserve of the human mind, devoid of any particularistic considerations which threaten the universality of legal principle. I speak namely of the separation between Church and State so necessary to achieve this aim. Thus far, this approach should prove uncontroversial. As regards our underpinning epistemology, there shall be a slight deviation from the (conventional, and arguably naïve) view that reason, usually depicted as Bayesian practical rationality, is the best characterization of this ultimate intellectual tool. Rather, reason is herein understood as a mode of judgment composed of processes best reflective of the holistic human nature and required in the formulation of ideal decisions, themselves determinable by the optimality of their consequences. This is necessarily different from classical understandings of rationality as utility-maximization *not* because the end is different, but rather the means employed. For, it is unthinkable that any sensible moral theory applied collectively—let alone individually—may be practicable if divorced from, or contrary to, the fabric of our emotional and corporeal constitution. Uncompromising moral edicts, when the product solely of thought in a vacuum, are destined to fail at the crossroads of theory and practice.

While this epistemological method does not ultimately prove crucial in understanding the ethical conclusions to be derived, it is nevertheless helpful in viewing the holistic enterprise of ethics and law as subjects incapable of exclusion from our psychology, as opposed to languishing exclusively under the auspices of hermetic pedantry. Duly, reason may be understood as comprising not only rational elements, but too emotional and experiential modes of knowledge acquisition, each of which colors our understanding of moral value and obligation. This proves essential in concerning the idiographic nature of fairness as dependent upon taking into account circumstances of the individual case, rather than viewing justice solely through the prism of Aristotelian distributive justice. For instance, whereas rationality commands an ethical perspective marked by objectivity between parties rather than personal self-interest, one could hardly disregard that many of our most instinctive moral sensibilities are understood in terms of emotional proximity, rather than utilitarian calculation (*e.g.*, no devoted mother would frame her parental responsibilities in terms of overarching moral duty as opposed to simple love for her child, much as no rescuer coldly calculates the potential liability of his actions[1]). Similarly, there are those aspects of learning which fall into neither camp, and are only understood in terms of the grayscale of empirical experience. While this may not inform the content of moral rules explicitly, it is essential in delimiting the boundaries of their effective—namely legal—implementation. No man possesses infinite endurance or integrity, much as no theory, however artful on the page, may translate into real practice without some error. These are the teachings solely of experience, and vital in understanding that moral philosophy cannot ever altogether write out shortcomings—or need for individual discretionary judgment—on the part of man. The ascendance of this view is epitomized by the 19th century American school of Legal Realism, its mantra encapsulated by Oliver

---

1 *Haynes v Harwood* [1935] 1 KB 146

Wendell Holmes Jr.: "The life of the law has not been logic; it has been experience."[1]

Reason thus, guides our attempt at a successful, complete and yet simultaneously workable ethics as one which appeals to our rational, uniquely personal and seasoned facets. Exactly how each of these components is integrated shall be forthcoming, but cursorily, whereas rationality provides a basis for impartial axiological construction (and therefore most sympathetic to the flavor of deontological thinking), emotional awareness provides for a theory which does not disregard the jealous demands of individual justice in the name of the greater good (thereby inheriting the spirit of Aristotle's individual-centered philosophy), and experience serves to warn us that any model is only valuable if capable of actual *and* widespread application (no doubt utilitarianism best satisfies this criterion).

Before continuing, it is perhaps befitting to ask why any of this matters. How, pray tell, asks the man on the street, does the minutiae of such contemplation contribute meaningfully to the life of the individual? To society? To mankind itself? This is not a daft question, for apart from ensuring their own job security, too often philosophers—ethicists foremost amongst them—lose sight of the *practical import* of their ideas. Ethics serves as the root discipline of law because it best addresses the simplest and most important question of all: "How ought we to live amongst one another?"

Perspectival Bias

Different schools of thought in ethics hold different vantage points. Not all, if any, can be valid if we are not to first streamline, let alone unify, this field of possibilities. We shall begin with deontology, which in its adherence to fixed principles independent of the contrivance of man, is firmly grounded on the "experiential" side of what I term the *rational/experiential impasse*. That is, deontology views the individual as its reconnoiterer, viewing his

---

1 *The Common Law*, 5, 1881

reports as the basis of moral consideration. Consequentialism, on the other hand, adopts a bird's-eye approach, viewing agents "top-down" as competing interests rather than from any single subjective perspective. Ironically, it is this allegedly aloof disposition which ultimately proves most sympathetic to the dignity of the individual. However, let us turn first to the "bottom-up" approach taken by deontologists. To reify these concepts, let us employ Foot's classic trolley problem, where she writes:

> Suppose the driver of a runaway tram can only steer from one narrow track on to another; five men are working on one track and one man on the other; anyone on the track he enters is bound to be killed.[1]

Adopting a traditional deontological prohibition on killing, one which would forbid the ending of a life under any circumstances, this dilemma could only be resolved by the driver *omitting* to deviate the path of the tram. Only by not positively influencing its course could he remain unblameworthy (this is woefully problematic, however, especially as regards legal—in addition to moral—culpability, as discussed later). More relevant, though, is deontology's specific regard to the preservation of an individual life, even at the expense of a potentially greater number (*e.g.*, if the tram was presently on course to strike five people, rather than one, the driver would be under the same duty not to alter its direction). A panoply of arguments support this position by deontological apologists, ranging from the irreducible dignity of a single life (that is, a value which cannot simply be traded off in a perverse game of numbers) to the discreteness of conscience experience (that subjective being is an unfungible quality incapable of utile reduction or transplantation to another).[2] Cumulatively, these arguments betray an *experiential*

---

1 Philippa Foot, 'The Problem of Abortion and the Doctrine of the Double Effect in Virtues and Vices'. *Oxford Review*, Number 5, 1967.
2 That 'utilitarianism does not take seriously the distinction between persons' (27) was first prominently addressed by Rawls in his 1971 treatise *A Theory of Justice*.

bias—one which views the uniqueness of individual conscious-ness as justification for its constituting the ultimate boundary of ethical concern. Such is why deontologists would forbid even hugely beneficial actions toward a worthy mass if at the expense of the unavoidable harm to a single innocent individual; they would argue that the harm faced by that one individual is not less significant than the benefit received by any one of the many, not least because the benefit received by the group could only be understood at an individual level. Whilst preliminarily difficult to argue with the logic inherent in this position, the dire costs endemic in its implementation render deontology an unviable system (moreover, there are purely philosophical difficulties it fails to convincingly overcome).

Rather, we must turn to the *rational* focus of consequential-ism, and, because of its agent-neutrality, utilitarianism in par-ticular, for the viewpoint of the administration of justice cannot be but impartial. While this school is ripe for criticism as a de-humanizing undertaking, one which reduces individuals to their respective hedonic outputs, its status as the default schema by which widespread decision-making is guided—in fields as di-verse as military tactics to economic and public policy—cannot be ignored. The reason being that utilitarianism maintains a su-perb grasp on the reality of interpersonal social interaction: that individuals exist with competing interests amidst a backdrop of *scarce utile resources.* Accordingly, there must be an objective and impartial means by which these conflicting pursuits ought to be prioritized; whereas deontology is often unwilling to engage in so tawdry an enterprise, consequentialism is fortunately not so inflexible. In doing so, utilitarianism necessarily adopts an *extra-*personal viewpoint, one situated beyond the confines of individ-ual awareness and therefore capable of *inter*personal regulation. This can be seen if we return to the trolley problem, whereby *ce-teris paribus* (*i.e.,* the unfortunate souls positioned along the track are similar to one another in age, health, utile output, etc.) the driver is not only permitted, but *obligated,* to deviate to the track with fewest persons—in this case, a single man.

The rationale supporting this course of action recognizes that in an imperfect situation in which *all relevant moral interests cannot be satisfied*, there must be a scheme employable that provides actionable resolution. This can only be understood by stepping away from the individual, and viewing agents as negotiable commodities capable of fungible treatment, the common denominator between them their capacity for utile consumption and production, utility itself best understood as legitimate preference satisfaction, or the pleasures normally obtainable without infringing on the ability of others to do similarly. This is what is meant by adopting a rational third-person perspective, as opposed to the experience-centric approach advocated by deontology designed to preserve the alleged dignity intrinsic to being. A perverse irony therefore follows that this quality is oftentimes most jeopardized by deontology's failure to provide practical solutions, owing to its equivocation of the *unfungibility of consciousness* with the very real ability to meaningfully *collate utility within and between individual*—albeit discrete—*lives.* Simply because subjective consciousness cannot be aggregated hardly affects the high value still placed upon it by its bearer. In fact, such only goes to prove that the maximization of life (or more specifically, its utile quality) is an absolute good—again, not because subjective pleasure is a quality capable of commensurate exchange, but rather because it is a good for the subject himself, and that any multiplication of this state of affairs is preferable to one in which it is reduced or altogether absent. That a man is the only one who can savor his own happiness is immaterial to the fact that a greater number tendered this fate is to be welcomed over any lesser number.

All of this necessarily leads to our preferring the consequentialist third-person perspective to the first-person viewpoint of deontology (also shared with virtue ethics with its strong emphasis on the unique personal characteristics of the moral agent). Toward this end, the law acts as a crucible in which civic values are nurtured on the individual, subjective level, and yet adjudged according to the demands of universal objectivity through the impartial channels of the judiciary.

Two Sovereign Masters

As he so incisively introduced in his *Principles of Morals and Legislation* over two centuries ago, Jeremy Bentham correctly identified the ultimate moral criteria of human action:

> Nature has placed mankind under the governance of two sovereign masters, pain and pleasure. It is for them alone to point out what we ought to do, as well as to determine what we shall do. On the one hand the standard of right and wrong, on the other the chain of causes and effects, are fastened to their throne. They govern us in all we do, in all we say, in all we think...[1]

Much as Thucydides foresaw the repetition of historical events to be a function of the unchanging human nature, so too are the foundations of moral law equally constant, themselves a function of our innate gravitation toward pleasure and aversion to pain in all their forms. Resultantly, pleasure is the only moral good. Of course, so contestable a claim cannot be made offhand, and requires ample defense. Toward this end, it is not likely that the claim "pleasure is *a* moral good" should find many critics, but rather that it is the "only" good. Even so, as Epicurus noted over two millennia ago, sustained pleasure is synonymous with the *eudaimon* lifestyle as one of happiness, which, per the earlier writings of Aristotle, was viewed to be the only incontrovertible aim that all humans pursued as an end in itself. We can only view society as the necessary organization which seeks the most efficient manifestation of this individually sought-after end. We must ask ourselves if there are truly *no* other candidates for our axiology. Is society driven toward an end apart from hedonic flourishing? It is fair to say that most laymen, and many philoso-

---

1 1789, 'Of the Principle of Utility'.

phers, would respond in the affirmative, citing a slew of candidates including truth, loyalty, love and, perhaps most widely, autonomy (values all similarly enshrined in virtue ethics)—any of which they might claim rivals, if not exceeds, pleasure in importance as a moral aspiration.

While it is beyond the scope of our piece to address each of these in turn, we shall content ourselves by rebutting human freedom as the most promising alternative to pleasure as a central moral value. All other purported qualities are herein considered either to be unfounded or, as in the case of the aforesaid, instances of rule utilitarianism—that is, not moral goods unto themselves but merely capable of producing pleasure. Their success toward this end has led to their historical conflation as goods in and of themselves, rather than merely utile rules (e.g., it is implausible that an unnecessarily hurtful statement—say, a disparagement of a leper's appearance—even if true, is ethically justified, much as love cannot be sustained without some form of utile compensation, such as affection or tangible nurturing in the guise of temporal and material effort expended on behalf of another). Of course, it is noteworthy that the difference between deontological and utilitarian theories is nevertheless often exaggerated, for both appeal to the idea of morally-inherent values; whereas for the former they include a wide variety of candidates, the latter confines itself to pleasure. Duly, the object of utilitarianism is irreducibly concerned with the maximization of an inherent good, albeit one whose efficacy is assessed by virtue of the scale of its impact rather than devout obedience to upholding the good itself regardless of its effects. Similarly, deontology (much like generalized aretaic character traits) may be understood as a subset of consequentialism, or more specifically a special form of rule utilitarianism. All deontological rules are only sensible as moral constructs if aimed at achieving a particular *end*; for only in relation to the tangible consequence of an act is its innate desirability (or lack thereof) made known to us.

Let us return to a value especially prized by deontology—human freedom. An unexpectedly fruitful approach toward diffus-ing the arguments made by those lauding autonomy as the chief moral value is to reverse-engineer one of their most relied upon thought experiments, the celebrated "Experience Machine" con-ceived by libertarian philosopher Robert Nozick.[1] In it, he poses that scientists of the future have developed a device capable of simulating any desirable stimuli, communicable directly to our brain. If connected, the subject would be fed an endless stream of pleasing sensations, though at the cost of freedom, in effect becoming a mind-slave to the machine. He then makes the rath-er presumptuous leap that most people would not accept such a fate but would instead prefer a life marred even extensively by unhappiness, if one nevertheless characterized by uninfringed autonomy. Both the claim that most would reject this oppor-tunity, and the reasons behind such a decision, are vigorously disputed.

For Nozick and others, there is great value to the "realness" of life, even if that mandates the experience of frustration and pain, because autonomy is inherently valuable, not least as a prerequisite for moral agency. While this last point is heartily conceded, the assumed value of such autonomy in and of itself is misguided. Cursorily, one may argue that there is great signifi-cance in this ability; not only does it separate us from predomi-nantly instinct-driven animals and provide us the capacity for reason, it is also the source of the richness of individuality and what many think of as an "authenticity of self." All of these argu-ments are plausible, and the latter statements seem intuitively obvious. That, however, does not address the more pressing concern of both the ultimate value and function of autonomy: *what is it good for?* This question presupposes that autonomy ex-

---

1 *Anarchy, State, and Utopia* (1974). 42–45. Autonomy is amongst the fore-most values which must be upheld in the administration of justice. This is not in dispute here; rather, the philosophical legitimacy of autonomy as a moral essence in itself is. This, however, for reasons forthcoming, proves irrelevant in the *functional* aims of the law, much as respect for 'natural' rights proves a necessary legal fiction, justified on utilitarian, as opposed to metaphysical, grounds.

isting just for itself is unsatisfactory (unlike with pleasure, its own and complete good). Is this the case? Well, consider this: imagine a man is granted full freedom of thought and action, and yet his life is marked by more misery than happiness—is such a life worth living? Is the authenticity of being a homeless beggar, crippled by hunger, valuable? Or a wealthy industrialist tormented by depression? How about the lifestyle of a perfectly average man, suffering from no ailments or hardship but simply bored to tears by daily existence? This question draws into sharp relief the actual value of autonomy, for beyond serving as a means to an end, where is its value? What benefit do we actually glean from merely the *capacity* for free action—the very definition of autonomy?

The answer is surprisingly little, if any. Instead, we value autonomy because, there existing no such thing as an Experience Machine, we must confine ourselves to pursuing happiness by our own devices, through the mechanism of autonomy. While the prospect of having our pleasures spoon-fed to us (as through the Machine) would be preferable, failing that, it is we who must actively pursue them through self-initiated action (via autonomy). If we accept that life has no predetermined meaning forged in the cosmos, then its highest function exists in the experience of pleasure, the only intrinsic good. But how can we make the assertion that we value autonomy only for the pursuit of pleasure? Consider this: we do not seek autonomy for its own sake, unlike pleasure. Autonomy is not pursued as an end; it is merely the means toward something else. There is no value in the *potential* to do something; *value is meaningful only if tangibly achieved or personally experienced*. Nothing can have value devoid of qualitative meaning, so in order for this not to be the case, it must therefore be prone to sentient understanding or experience.

Therefore, we can understand autonomy as an empty pursuit, for its value is not self-contained. Rather, it is valuable only because it is instrumental in achieving another value, that being pleasure. If one accepts this argument, then Nozick appears mistaken in believing that one would not willingly accept pleasure freely provided by an Experience Machine, especially since it is done so with "minimal costs" to the individual.[1] To think more clearly about this issue, imagine we were *born* as a subject within the Experience Machine. In such a case, if offered autonomy with the guarantee of less pleasure, how many would opt for that? I would imagine few, if any, for those in possession of pleasure appear rather jealous of its continued relish. What, then, would prompt Nozick, and admittedly so many others, to opt for autonomy over pleasure? Though the answer is not obvious, it is most likely a combination of not exhausting reason to its furthest conclusions, intuitive fears about forfeiting autonomy in light of the unknown versus maintaining a *status quo* bias, to even possibly entrenched religious inculcations, however allegedly ignored, which traditionally sanctify the dignity accordant with human freedom. Of note, however, is the understanding that the Machine in question can perfectly simulate *any* human experience, and that once connected, the subject is unaware he is so.[2] Thus, any reticence based on the simple unthinkability of

---

1 'Minimal costs' refer to the Experience Machine providing pleasure without effort required by the individual, compared to the individual who, granted with autonomy, would have to effortfully pursue such pleasure in real life. As experience teaches us, such latter pursuit is never perfectly efficient in hedonic terms, meaning that total pleasure could never be experienced without the accompanying non-zero presence of displeasure insofar as the effort required to attain it. Because autonomy has been shown to have no value in itself and has higher utile costs than connecting oneself to the Experience Machine, such strongly suggests that any rational agent would willingly forfeit the former for the latter.

2 Intuitively, we may think of the Experience Machine as replicating only physical, as opposed to intellectual and emotional, pleasures. Nothing lends itself to suggest this conclusion. This misguided view may however be explicable because we tend to view physical pleasures as requiring the least proactivity on our part, instead being capable of passive enjoyment. Relative to intellectual and emotional pleasures, this seems somewhat true; for example, a massage provides inactive pleasure relative to the more durable joys of scrutinizing Plato. Nevertheless, all pleasures require active engagement to some extent; even the physical requires the mental willingness to experience it (*e.g.*, one cannot enjoy a massage unless he clears his mind to do so, much as one cannot enjoy sex unless an enthused participant), albeit less than other types, namely the intellectual and emotional.

surrendering the very quality which typifies the human experi-ence—capacity for thought and action—are upon closer, braver and less dogmatic examination, ungrounded. For the Machine does not provide mere simulacra but a virtual world indistin-guishable from external reality, via experiences which define our conception of the latter.

No one can convincingly justify the superiority of our pres-ent reality over one in which universal happiness was achiev-able, even if at the cost of the absence of individual agency and moral desert. For in recognizing happiness to be the only good, the value of freedom is but an inescapable and necessary delu-sion, one which we must be resigned to accept with stoic grace in the absence of a better alternative. Herein lies the practical necessity of autonomy, and one which cannot be ignored by even the most imaginative juridical sophistry; that a man is per-sonally responsible for the acts he commits and must face the consequences accordingly. Notwithstanding this taxing misfor-tune, the aforesaid argument lends philosophical certitude to the proposition that pleasure is the sole moral good and must therefore be upheld by any legitimate ethical theory. In view of this, we are unsurprised to find in utilitarianism an especially kindred spirit.

Sense upon Stilts

By now, we have laid the groundwork for presenting our unified theory, having first discounted both the axiologies and perspectives which underpin the alternatives. Toward this end, we are ready to supply the preliminary content of our ethics, beginning with perhaps the central fixture of contemporary meta-ethics—the default presumption of the existence of rights. While faith in their inseparability from the human nature is ro-bust amongst thinkers and laymen alike, such belief cannot go unchallenged. As we are dealing with a materialistic ethics, it is conceded that rights are a noble fiction, a contrivance of man necessary to develop a common system of interpersonal respect which makes possible the stable administration of society. They are quite simply not part of the "fabric of the world",[1] as other natural features, such as the laws of physics or material objects, might be. However, so as not to take so bleak a view as Bentham in his famous pronouncement of natural rights as "nonsense upon stilts",[2] they must be understood, like any deontological prescription, to be merely utile rules, and hence ultimately capable of being overridden under exceptional circumstances—namely, those in which not *all rights may be satisfied* due to either their competing objectives or logistical constraints. Any violation must not exceed the minimal extent required for the protection of the greatest interest as assessed in terms of both quality and quantity, such that a partial disregard of rights is to be preferred prior to an otherwise total disregard. Seldom will so grave a forced choice be thrust upon us, however, for in actuality the neglect of rights (most egregiously manifested in society via conscription or torture techniques used in interrogation) is only justified under the severest threat to the very socioethical framework first responsible for granting rights to its subjects—such as a war of existential proportions against the nation-state. Contempt for rights prior to crossing this threshold endangers both the moral legitimacy and civic support of all apparatuses of the state. So, if we are ultimately resigned to view rights as nonsense, let us instead view them as useful nonsense.

Despite metaphysically "fixed" rules not being in place within our moral system does not exclude the existence of very real, albeit relatively utile, ones—the most prominent of which is justice as defined as *hedonic reciprocity*, itself the balancing of the utile outcomes between two or more parties. This includes both the actors' intentions[3] and the magnitude of the consequences of

---

1 JL Mackie. 'The Subjectivity of Values', *Ethics: Inventing Right and Wrong* (1977).
2 'A Critical Examination of the Declaration of Rights', *Anarchical Fallacies* (1843).
3 While intent is critical in the determination of individual justice, it is nevertheless far more difficult to assess than the tangible impact of one's actions. Consequently, in matters of practically determining eq-

their actions. Justice therefore, is a median upon a hedonic continuum assessing the nature of interpersonal behavior, centered between the two extremes of mercy (or undue reward) and cruelty (or undue punishment). It serves as the focal point of our axiology not merely owing to its perspective of agent-neutrality (that is, the impartial ascertainment of fairness between parties, rather than subjective bias in favor of one over another), but because it recognizes the practical limitations of any moral theory derived from considerations of pleasure. This is to say that justice as the baseline of moral obligation stems from its appreciation of the scarcity of utile resources, and that for every act of consumption there is a necessary shortage—limited supply for unlimited demand. Accordingly, it requires that every man pay the adequate price for his pleasure, usually in the expenditure of some form of labor. This is further necessary considering that no man is an island, and almost every source of utility is a function of social interdependence at some level; the butcher nor brewer nor baker offers his services without due recompense, and the bartering of proportionate labors between parties ensures the absence of injustice expressed as utile exploitation.

There is another, perhaps more powerful, implication in justice as the ultimate utilitarian value. If we recognize pleasure as its own good, and the maximization of its experience as necessarily desirable, then the appeal of utilitarianism is striking. However, there is an immediate tension between this ideal goal and the very practical constraints of resource limitation. Not all wants can be satisfied, and not all pleasures may be enjoyed. This is where justice makes its entrance; it is the great filter separating hedonic desert from the mere unworthy wanting of pleasure. Toward this end, our "meritocratic utilitarianism" in

uity, we must often look to the magnitude of one's actions in determining their due response, assuming that actions mirror intentions in the absence of contrary evidence. This assumption takes on especial importance as regards the burden of proof in civil and criminal trials, where the defendant's actions (barring some defense invoking mistake or loss of voluntary control) are taken to be the direct manifestation of his will.

short expresses the novel idea that one ought to maximize plea-sure for the greatest number, *proceeding in descending order of priority from the highest utile producers.*[1] This important modification of clas-sical utilitarianism preserves the conventional aim to maximize quantitative experience of the Good, but not at the expense of sacrificing justice in individual cases, whereby the greatest utile producers are to be rewarded first for the fruits of their labor which benefit not only themselves, but society at large. Whilst some might decry this bifurcation of moral entitlement between the "more" and "less" meritorious (perhaps even likening it to a slippery slope by which justice may become hijacked as a defense of elitist indulgence), its advocacy herein is based not upon inherent desirability but rather practical necessity, for in a world in which utile resources are all too often severely limited in supply, it is only individual merit as measured by utile output which may serve to not only justly regulate their distribution, but further augment their production—for in the utile output of society's most successful members is frequently incurred signifi-cant input of utile resources.

Rarely will so stark a dilemma exist that individual justice shall conflict with achieving the greater good. However, it can-not be said that such instances are unknown to the law, at least where the aforementioned two aims conflict in part if not en-tirely. The widespread use of plea bargains in criminal proceed-ings illustrates the power of utilitarian logic in the exercise of prosecutorial discretion, such that a "minor" defendant will be exonerated so as to provide material evidence against a far more public and/or dangerous mastermind. Such thinking colors the civil law as well, where the wrongful acts of company directors (such as when in breach of the powers conferred upon them by the corporate constitution) can be retrospectively ratified by shareholders if deemed to be in the best interests of the com-pany (e.g., securing a lucrative contract which will raise share

---

1 Here, 'highest' producers is firstly concerned with the qualitative su-periority of the utile output, followed by its quantitative maximization.

prices and benefit the members collectively). In such cases, the director is shielded from personal liability, notwithstanding his breaches. Equally, in equity, the unauthorized dissemination of capital under a trust may "cheat" the beneficiaries of their due entitlement, yet be unrecoverable if innocent third parties either relied upon or spent such funds in good faith, as was the case in *Re Diplock* (1948), where unwitting recipient charities used such money to pay off debts and repair property.

A Hierarchy of Pleasure

Thus far, we have made much progress in defending utilitarianism (albeit somewhat modified) as the best candidate for a coherent ethical system, not only because of its sound axiology but also its unique capacity to subsume rival theories' objectives as extensions of rule utilitarianism. However, our task does not end here, for in delineating our meritocratic utilitarianism we must further take into account calculations involving the *quality* of utile output, in addition to its mere quantitative maximization. In doing so, our understanding of pleasure necessarily adopts a Millian flair, which, however complicating, remains necessary if we are to precisely understand the multifarious nature of pleasure. Specifically, no utilitarian theory can accurately prioritize utile obligations without separating the wheat from the chaff—that is, via the construction of a hierarchy of pleasure.

Unlike the one described by Mill, however, ours is a reflection of the tripartite nature of reason itself, comprised of rational, emotional and experiential components. Whilst he focused on a qualitative separation based upon aesthetic judgment pursuant to personal experience (*e.g.,* anyone exposed to football and Socratic discourse could not help but prefer the latter),[1] we have not so much faith in the promise of individual discernment. Rather, our hierarchy is justified on two distinct grounds; first, the relative *durability* of differing types of utility (namely intellectual, emotional and physical) and second, its *actualization po-*

1 'What Utilitarianism Is,' *Utilitarianism* (1863)

tential. The first criterion refers to the extent to which any utile typology is vulnerable to perishability, such as through the passage of time or an external locus of causation outside of one's own control. The imperviousness of a given pleasure becomes synonymous with its immunity to external degradation. Accordingly, intellectual pleasures must assume priority as they concern the most inextricable aspect of the human persona—our unique ways of interpreting the world around us, which include the capacity for adopting any nondescript utile-maximizing set of behaviors across a wide spectrum of circumstances. They permit the internalization of knowledge which itself forms personality and calibrates our very outlook on life, critically important because of its independence from the ephemerality of external events (especially so when negative). Emotional pleasures inescapably necessitate codependence upon others and, while they are oftentimes intense and deeply affirming, nevertheless entail a departure from the full autonomy otherwise maintained under the command of self-referential intellect. Nowhere is the danger of utility being dependent upon a source external to oneself more striking that in the case of love—a firmly emotional pleasure—for it jeopardizes the very autonomy which is the seat of agency itself. Once autonomy is compromised in favor of some form of external reliance, there is no limit to the lengths taken to pursue pleasure, including the forfeiture of moral duty. Injustice of this variety must always be too high a price to pay for our pleasure. Unsurprisingly, pleasures of the flesh prove the most fleeting, and should be duly accorded the lowest priority. Our second criterion sheds light on the unique nature of man relative to other members of the animal kingdom. What separates our species chiefly from barbarism is the application of reason—the epitome of our actualization potential—and this is fittingly reflected in the aforesaid hierarchy: the intellect represents the most innately "human" activity, emotion our somewhat less unique capacity for fraternal intercourse, and brute physicality proves no different from the kind demonstrated by any other sentient being.

The usefulness of any hedonic hierarchy in assigning moral priorities should not be construed too widely. For, despite the above ranking holding steadfastly true when all species of pleasure are in equal supply, it transforms into a sliding scale when conditions are otherwise. As a result, an inferior pleasure may become more valuable owing to its relative scarcity, though this does not necessarily imply that the *entirety* of a higher (albeit more abundant) form of pleasure may be traded for a lesser one; there exists a bounded, absolute threshold which may not be crossed. Imagine a national politician seeking to defund all state sponsorship of the arts so as to renovate football stadiums across the country. Whilst this measure might prove immensely popular with voters, it would nevertheless prove morally impermissible[1] as it would discourage the societal cultivation of those values most uplifting to its citizenry. Another function of our hierarchy exists in its encouraging the diversification of pleasure, for it identifies the wide array of activities ripe for enjoyment. Whereas the over- or underexposure to any pleasing undertaking is likely to yield a suboptimal imbalance, a hierarchy of pleasure is designed specifically to avoid this eventuality. Its purpose is not the elimination of lower forms of pleasure, but simply their lesser prioritization relative to higher forms. In doing so, boredom becomes an impossibility, and life a continuous surge of new and delighting discoveries.

Altogether, utilitarianism cannot survive as either an intelligible or credible model without the inclusion of considerations of the qualitative *and* quantitative dimensions of utility. This union forges an even deeper degree of consilience on multiple levels, the first being the fusion of deontological and aretaic

---

1 That it would be legally possible reflects the distinct aims of these fields. In the case of law, popular consensus must ultimately prove the means by which political and legislative action are justified, regardless of their departure from an objective moral code. To arrange the body politic otherwise would be to impose an elitist worldview upon an unwilling majority which would make impossible the effective administration of government.

principles as expressions of uniquely important pleasures (*i.e.*, expressed as utile rules). For instance, the deontological proscription on using others instrumentally is expressed in qualitative terms by the prioritization of the intellect (itself the best expression of personal autonomy) over the physical—that is, to enslave an erstwhile academic into a position of forced labor is morally forbidden since tantamount to the reduction of a noble creature to the status of a mindless animal. Consilience occurs on yet another level, that of permitting individual justice as regards the rewarding of utile resources to individuals whose merit is not to be measured first by bulk but rather by the caliber of their actions. This qualitative–quantitative fusion thereby ensures the meritocratic basis of this type of utilitarianism, providing unification such that the beginnings of a model of justice that is both intellectually rigorous and practicable emerge.

Miscellaneous Issues

Before distilling our key findings, we shall consider certain tangential, albeit refining, points. These shall include the roles played by *intent, omission* and *hedonic quantification* within our conceptual framework. As regards intent, it is too true that the consequences of an action alone, regardless of premeditation, render the realm of moral judgment nothing more than a roulette wheel of reward and punishment, with no agent responsible for his actions owing to the absence of forethought. Equally, the complete disregard of the consequences of an act similarly leaves ethics an impotent science—one relegated to the realm of desire and not achievement, cause but not effect. Good intentions by themselves do not make a good deed, but rather the latter is a result of a combination of the will and the body, the intent and its corresponding action. Framed in negative terms, this is analogous to the dual legal requirements of *mens rea* and *actus reus* in establishing criminal culpability. Both the forethought found in intent and its actionable manifestation are necessary for full moral judgment to occur—indeed, it may be said that no choice is expressed at all unless constitutive of both components. If so, then ethicists face the conundrum of defining the relationship between motive and outcome. Presently, any proposed explanation proves less than wholly satisfying.

Until the forlorn day in which even the privacy of thought becomes a relic of a gentler time—a prospect made not unthinkable by the unrelenting march of pervertible science—it shall be impossible to know with certainty the allegiances of a man's conscience. Therefore we are left to assume, except where sufficient evidence suggests contrariwise, that it is the character of the action itself which provides insight into prior intent. In the judicial context, we may add witness and documentary testimony to the observable behaviors of the defendant. We should affix to this rule of thumb the proviso that in times of palpable uncertainty, whereupon the intent simply cannot be ascertained even from the residual effects of action, a suspect should be provided the benefit of the doubt, for it seems the greater crime to punish the guiltless and produce a clear harm than to forgo the punishment of even those guilty parties whose crimes, having already injured, cannot be reversed through the zealotry of vengeful justice.

Omission, contrary to popular belief, is qualitatively identical to positive action; it possesses both intent and tangible consequences. To therefore classify omission as a special class of action—one excused from normal moral considerations—is fundamentally misguided. Omission, like with all deontological rules, is only desirable because it achieves some consequence (even if that is the absence of an otherwise proscribed act). Deontology itself collapses into a special form of consequentialism, for even the most intuitive moral laws are only valuable not in the abstract, but because they achieve some end which is sensibly beneficial to us. Omission is no different; it attempts to achieve some end, either by adherence to an abstract principle or because it plainly attempts to prevent some tangible harm. The end result is an insoluble problem for deontologists—unlike utilitarians, who deal in matters of preferentially relative, as opposed to absolute, courses of action—in that the unavailability of omission as a valid moral option prevents their subjects from functioning altogether in any scenario in which there is no straightforward moral course of action (such as in the trolley problem, where killing is forbidden and yet unavoidable even through omission; foresight of certain death prevents it from truly circumventing the deontological prohibition on ending life). Such a lacuna is illustrative of a unique flaw in this school of thought, yet one rectifiable by consequentialism owing to the absence of any blanket prohibitions on certain behaviors.

The legal consequences of omission, however, have long been held distinct from its moral blameworthiness. It is an enshrined legal principle that barring a relationship of reliance (whether through contract, as a fiduciary or filialness), there is no general duty to act for the benefit of another. Of course, the decision to do so may incur liability, especially where a well-intentioned Samaritan inadvertently makes a situation worse. Is the absence of an overriding duty to act legally justifiable? The law, with its schizophrenic allegiances between deontological and consequentialist logic, clearly prefers the former in this case. It is tortuously difficult to defend this position, at least when taken to its logical extreme.[1] Imagine a bystander sunning himself on a deserted beach, when suddenly are heard cries for help from a drowning victim in the sea. Though a competent and strong swimmer, our onlooker decides not to act, and, with no one else around, watches on as the helpless victim predictably disappears beneath the waterline, dies. According to the law, he was under no duty to save this man, but can we intellectually—let alone morally—defend this? I say no, for reasons not only philosophical but consistent with the practical aims of the law. For its purpose is not only the stable administration of competing

---

1 In fact, a "duty of easy rescue" is not unknown in certain countries, such as France and Germany, where the deliberate failure to provide assistance to a person in peril may be punishable by imprisonment and/or a fine.

interests within society, but per Lord Devlin, the "enforcement of morals." Whilst this thesis is misguidedly considered the antithesis of the assumptions underpinning classical liberalism, it actually recognizes that there is an irreducible sociocultural legacy which both informs and is informed by the substance of law. Accordingly, one cannot divorce from its axiology prevailing norms. We are embarking on a new and unprecedented age, one where the law has struck a balance between the atomistic individualism of an unrestrained Victorian liberalism and the robust social ethos fostered across disparate legal fields—from the explosion in the number of tortious duties of care to the enforcement of minimal standards of human rights in international law. Ironically, in the wake of globalization, ideas of an international connectedness have never been stronger, and yet domestic legal frameworks have consistently encouraged the social fragmentation of individual duty to one's fellow citizens through the elimination of criminalizing arguably other-regarding acts. A prime example is the decriminalization of homosexuality in Britain following the Wolfenden report in 1957. While it is today anathema in most quarters to consider homosexual behavior apt for legal sanction, not least because it is engaged in consensually, the eventual erosion of homophobia can be explained as adequately through evolving cultural norms as through the forced Millian liberalism which originally supported its legalization. For, the underbelly of this line of thinking is to divorce from individual citizens a civic responsibility to their peers and polis. The law cannot exist in a vacuum such that it does not seek to provide the most basic moral education to its citizenry, for while the thrust of this duty is placed upon the family unit, their failure in executing this charge seldom renders the State unwilling to prosecute those who offend its laws. *Ignorantia juris non excusat.*

Let us return to our dishonorable sunbather. There are two primary arguments as to why his inaction should yield liability, followed by an important qualification. His duty to act is, first and foremost, a moral duty: it is that of justice, insofar as justice is maximized hedonic reciprocity, further accounting for higher qualitative pleasures to be rewarded prior to lower ones. This instance invokes justice because the utile demand made upon our sunbather is minimal, and, per the limited data we have been given, the victim is nominally "worthy" of having his life saved. As morality is the rock upon which the administrative edifice of law is built, the values the latter seeks to uphold are ultimately inseparable from moral justification. Second, enforcement of this duty fulfills a sociological function beyond the mere facilitation of non-aggression amongst members of society. It communicates a positive statement as to the symbiosis of civic existence; that failure to aid one in mortal peril should be admonished not solely owing to its moral reprehensibility, but the disintegrating effect it has upon community. That individuals owe no obligations to each other renders the benefits of society negligible; rather than a civilizing forum in which the sensibilities of man are refined, it instead becomes a useful means of maximizing self-interest, a hyper-efficient marketplace. Of course, there are grave concerns which follow the imposition of a general duty toward one's fellow man. How should this duty be circumscribed, for clearly one cannot be expected to aid everyone who is in need at every waking moment? And what if there are competing demands made of us in a given situation, only some of which can be satisfied?

These questions, like with so much of the preserve of naysayers generally, are not nearly as important as they appear in deterring actual practice. For every constructive proposal, there are drawbacks whose minutiae can render it a seemingly futile aim. For every new legal obligation, there is the inevitable "floodgates" argument. Not every slippery slope is slid down, and the imposition of a general duty in times of peril is one such case. If our sunbather were forced to choose between saving his drowning autistic sister or a Nobel laureate, and chose the former, then for the law to impose liability would be absurd; there are limits as to what may be expected from the consciences of men, notwithstanding the higher utility derivable from the latter victim. Such would be a moral mandate (albeit contentious), but not a legal one. However, it is another matter altogether to obliterate a minimal duty to save at least one of those drowning, if not both. The imposition of this duty is but the mildest extension of other responsibilities the law places upon us: the duty to not harm others, to not behave negligently, to act loyally in the position of a fiduciary. In fact, the mere existence of strict liability for certain activities independent of fault colors our modest proposal as seemingly wholly reasonable. That the law imposes a blanket exemption on any positive duty to act is implicitly justified under rule utilitarianism—that, while not desirable idiographically, it produces the best possible nomothetic outcome (*e.g.*, fewer bureaucratic demands placed upon the courts and police to handle cases of inaction, their time and attention instead dominated by overt infraction). However, in this alternate world, we are not asked to aid every man in distress nor to undertake particularly onerous or life-threatening risk; simply, we are asked to recognize that there is a generalized duty to behave reasonably toward the aid of another who is in peril, if possible.[1] For the law to deny this is for it to ignore its vital role in the ennobling socializing of man, in addition to its more conspicuous penal functions.

Undoubtedly, treating this duty with restraint follows from a key obstacle for any utilitarian: the quantification of competing hedonic priorities. That is, whose interests are more pressing: those of the industrialist responsible for running a massive factory (and hence overseeing many workers) or those of a single employee? Cursorily assuming the former, the question becomes both more significant and perplexing when calculating the relative interests of the industrialist and *all* of his employees collec

---

1 If this duty is never to arise in a court of law, then its nonexistence should be attributable to the logistical infeasibility of calculating the options open to bystanders when confronted by the imperilment of the victim in question, in addition to the laborious and necessarily inexact exercise required in reconstructing their decision-making calculus. It should not, however, be based upon any sophistical attempt to produce a principled justification for legally permitting inaction.

tively—which is greater now? Inevitably imperfect information of the situation proves this to be a perennial conundrum.[1] In this case, without further data, most would intuitively conclude the latter by sheer number. These problems of quantification, in relation to both the number affected and to what degree, are ameliorated by hedonic metrics such as intensity (the pleasure's strength), purity (whether any contrary sensation is present), duration, likelihood (of successfully achieving a desired end) and quality, the last of which refers to our aforementioned hierarchy of pleasure. Each of these hedonic metrics, the brainchild of Bentham's original felicific calculus,[2] admittedly proves difficult to numerate. While incapable of being transplanted onto an absolute scale, any rational attempt at quantification requires differing pleasures to be assigned numerical values according to their overall desirability (per the aforesaid metrics) as relative to one another. Similarly, there is a sliding scale which the courts must employ in balancing the conflicting aims of parties, especially when invoking the principle of proportionality, through which individual rights are minimally curtailed so as to make possible a superseding public aim.

A Moral Law?

For some time now, it has appeared fashionable for scholars across disciplines to suffer from "physics envy"—that is, the reductionist attempt by social scientists and humanists to mathematize or formulize their concepts. Philosophers have not proven immune to this trend. Whilst the present writer is not personally a proponent, it might be suggested that additional clarity may be gained in the elucidation of the interrelationship between the many concepts discussed via the concision of a single "moral law"—a statement of universal applicability to all

1 This is due to the asymmetry of information held by the state relative to individual actors in a given scenario, owing to the closer proximity to relevant facts and preferences enjoyed by the latter category.
2 'Value of a Lot of Pleasure or Pain, How to be Measured', *Principles of Morals and Legislation* (1789).

agents operating under any circumstances. Like the futility en-demic in any form of intellectual hubris, no grand unified theory wholly escapes qualification or lingering lacunae. Accordingly, what follows should best be understood as an approximate, albeit powerful, summary of the ethics herein advocated—a revised framework which provides not only theoretical consil-ience but a novel means of practical application, the wherewith-al to provide for the greater good as much as for justice in the individual case.

The Universal Moral Law:

> That which is moral requires the intended act of establishing equity—the balancing of the hierarchical utile natures of those actions between parties—toward the greatest number possible, whereby individual au-tonomy is held to be fundamentally sovereign unless such respect violates equity.

The above statement requires some explanation. Clearly, the touchstone of our meritocratic utilitarianism is achieving justice, or equity. However, not only is this requirement absent from classical utilitarianism (with its advocacy on the unre-stricted provision of pleasure), but so too is the primary empha-sis on the *qualitative* maximization of utility as a fixture of equity, quantitative maximization becoming a secondary priority. This nuance, the result of our divined hierarchy of pleasure, takes into account the individual character of man, allowing his fair due to be determined neither in a vacuum nor per the misunderstand-ing that the size of justness is one which can fit all. Intention fea-tures so as to convey the importance of premeditation as a func-tion of moral desert, however difficult the practical constraints in its measurement. Commentators might note with surprise the inclusion of considerations of autonomy in this law, especially following its excision from the list of relevant axiological values which ought to be upheld by any code of ethics. This would be a misreading, for, while autonomy is recognized not as an *inher-ent* moral good, it remains a practical necessity insofar as it is the conduit by which agency is manifested—it is the genesis of all self-directed action. This is relevant in moral terms owing to the interdependent nature of social existence. As almost no utile source exists beyond the purview of anthropogenic contrivance or manufacture, and such goods are invariably limited in supply but met with limitless demand, justice is the filter separating the worthy from the less so. Justice cannot be understood by us without appealing to the individual character of the actions of men, and such can only be deservedly rewarded if respectful for the free will—our autonomous capacity—which bore them.

The End We All Seek

Everything we have discussed would be moot if not for its role in finding happiness, the ultimate end of existence itself. All too frequently ethicists neglect the very essence which confers upon their discipline its status as the foremost of all human inquiries: its capacity to meaningfully better the life of man through the cultivation of value and character. Accordingly, ethical theories must not prove so abstruse as to defy daily implementation or to evade the comprehension of the common man. The same applies for legal reasoning; whereas a judicial elite are responsible for its crafting, its edicts must appear transparent and sensible to laymen. The framework propounded here is centrally concerned with human flourishing; not only is pleasure its singular aim, but framed between the contexts of individual just desert and maxi-mizing societal welfare. Striking an appropriate balance is at the forefront of any jurist's mind in rendering judgment, and such judgment cannot evade criticism, for reasons ranging from the irreducible arbitrary discretion involved to conflicting views as to whether individual rights should trump collective aims. Ulti-mately, the judiciary serves as much as a source of arbitral final-ity as it does a fountain of justice; impartiality is required in the pacific resolution of disputes, and decision-making *aporia* cannot be tolerated. The buck must stop somewhere, and, as with any human institution, this sentiment finds its expression in our courts of law: noble in intent, if at times frail in constitution. The relevance of virtue to the good life does not end in the realm of contemplation; it must be felt in the hearts of men and equally applied through the force of law, however imperfect. For, justness is the price of being worthy of happiness, not only as a functional prerequisite owing to the scarcity of utile resources but as the personal knowledge requiring that we first deem ourselves worthy of it before we may thereafter experientially enjoy its graces. This is the end we all seek, and yet it proves all too elusive for our liking. Let us hope our conclusions help to find a few more shards of this heaven for us all to savor.

Ethico-Legal Consilience

Never shall ethics and law perfectly coincide. This is partly due to the tawdry realities of social organization; man as a political animal cannot divorce any social structure from politics, and the law is no different. Considerations of populism, expediency, bias and corruption shall always constrain its reach of attaining the perfect embodiment of justice. Of course, political limitations realize themselves not solely via ethical shortcomings to achieve such lofty ends, but in the very structural determination of such ends in themselves. That is, justice is not the sole end of law; the ubiquity of logistical efficiency in the guise of procedure trumping substance rivals any moral precept in the contemplation of jurists' rulings, much as the precedential value of a case shapes its being decided on grounds independent of the merits of the individual facts, but rather taking account of its ramifications once universalized to all similar instances. These very real constraints ensure that jurists tend to treat law as the younger brother of ethics, unable to keep contemporaneous pace with the evolution of normative values. Notwithstanding this, ethics is the lynchpin of law, itself the codification of ethereal principle within an administrative apparatus. As such, the law is amongst the noblest professions, for not only does it require a mastery of rhetoric and a uniquely pragmatic and scholastic disposition but also the enforcement of morals, whose very content serves to maintain order and the cultural fabric of civilization itself.

Unlike ethics, the law therefore endures additional burdens. Its charge cannot be understood solely through the prism of ideality of thought, or even what is demanded of practical justice. Instead, law serves as a conduit for societal order and change, necessarily political objectives which may oft conflict with the immutable findings of ethical precepts. Therefore, any attempt to explain law as the mere sum of its constituent parts is to fail to realize its holistic, Gestaltian nature. However, the most promising avenue, both prescriptive and descriptive, in understanding law as a science is to adopt the approach first taken by the great utilitarians of the 19th century, thus having us follow in the wake of scholars such as Bentham, Mill and Austin. Explaining the *content*, as opposed to the superstructure or mechanisms for change, of the law necessarily invokes some consideration of utility, however initially counterintuitive by virtue of its cold pragmatism. Even offenses against the person, such as an unwarranted violation of bodily integrity, may be explained in utile terms (*e.g.*, a surgeon who performs an unauthorized and botched procedure rendering his patient paralyzed is liable because of the reduction in utility suffered relative to someone fully ambulatory). Of course, this utilitarian model is best expressed in the commercial, rather than criminal, sphere, even in anthropological terms.

Social organization is but the byproduct of utility-maximization; security, specialized goods, services and information are each more efficiently deliverable to the individual than in a prior state of Nature (or any anarcho-capitalist variation thereon). The law recognizes this fact and is, accordingly, predominantly concerned with the most seemingly "just" (itself a suspect term for "most utilely efficient") distribution of goods and services. It is resolving *this* perennial dilemma which produces the greatest intellectual wrangling amongst juridical scholars, not deciding upon the basic principles of justice of which the law is to uphold. Toward unraveling this knotty problem, however, are the aims of ethics and legal science most closely aligned.

How, then, are we to proceed from the justification of utilitarian thinking toward supplying the actual content of its obligations? A good place to start is understanding that, firstly, almost all utile goods—those resources which provide us pleasure (*e.g.*, food, building materials, books, technology, companionship, etc.)—are in limited supply relative to an unlimited demand, and secondly, that most such goods are the result of personal labor and therefore require a network of social interdependence. This requires that there be a suitable "give-and-take" in our daily interactions with others, for to exploit their labors without due compensation is to behave inequitably. Such is why the utmost principle of utilitarianism must be *justice*, or utile reciprocity between actors. Without this essential element, the incentive to produce diminishes, slowing the very engine which perpetuates social functioning. To claim utilitarianism demands only justice is a bit simplistic, for it is equally concerned with maximization of pleasure to the greatest number of people. But the overall idea becomes clear: at its broadest level of implantation, the law serves to facilitate the efficient distribution of vital utile goods so as to permit societal functioning, epitomized in the free exchange of goods and services. More narrowly, it regulates the specific terms of such transactions, such that agreements must conform to the protocols of fair-dealing and transparency, and whereupon they do not, whether through fraud, misrepresentation, duress or any other vitiating factor, such contracts are voidable.

The tripartite nature of reason was discussed earlier, and whilst perhaps an exemplar of philosophical thinking, also proves useful toward problem-solving and evidence-gathering within the legal realm. Constituent elements of this cognitive framework—namely, matters appertaining to experience and emotional awareness—may fuel justice in the specific case, especially through the demonstration of leniency from the bench when appropriate, much as judgments guided by policy considerations are influenced by the universality of rationalized directives. Of course, imbalances as regard the ideal calibration of these influencing factors undoubtedly abound, such as the importance of procedure even to the detriment of substantive justice inasmuch the logistical efficiency of an otherwise-overloaded docket is preserved. This should not make us fret overly, for law is, again, a very *human* construction, and therefore must be adjudged within the limits of reasonableness, just like any individual defendant on trial. Political interference and contested notions of the Good shall always render it a less than unchanging—let alone faultless—discipline, as will the selfish impulses of individual men. That is to say the law is unlikely to evolve beyond the point of self-interested concern, for any ethics which attempts to move beyond the teachings of liberalism is likely to prove incapable of legal translation. The answer is not obscure: any legal framework which prioritizes the collective good ahead of individual interest is likely to stop short upon encountering the rather mulish obstacle called human nature, even if such a framework is ethically sound. Sacrifice is the standard of martyrs and thus above the law, itself master to only laxer souls.

The nobler incarnations of law are nevertheless evident amidst its pragmatism if one observes closely, albeit in fields more often seen through the lens of idealism than the reality of their impact. I speak namely of constitutional and international law, two fields governed by the highest of moral influences and yet relatively unfaithful to the strict application of their guiding principles. The 18th century English case of *Entick v Carrington*[1]

---

1 [1765] EWHC KB J98. Ironically, despite the judgment in this English case signifying an important check upon governmental authority generally, its constitutional legacy was far better preserved in the United States where the ruling contributed to the enactment of the Fourth Amendment to the United States Constitution, which prohibits un-

proved an early vindication of individual privacy over the un-restrained exercise of executive authority, only to be—in prin-ciple, at least—run roughshod over by the unflinching doctrine of parliamentary sovereignty affirmed via the doctrine of implied repeal in *Ellen Street v Minister of Health*[1] almost two centuries later. The ramifications of the latter case reinforced the view that Par-liament had no legal master, and its legislation was confined to no moral limits beyond the collective conscience of its members, such that any prior legal restraint of political power could be removed at will. It was not until the 21st century that the earliest suggestion of a hierarchy of statutes gained prominence, albeit *obiter dictum*, in the Metric Martyrs case,[2] wherein Laws LJ stated:

> In the present state of its maturity the common law has come to recognize that there exist rights which should properly be classified as constitutional or fun-damental...We should recognise a hierarchy of Acts of Parliament: as it were "ordinary" statutes and "constitu-tional" statutes...[a] constitutional statute is one which (a) conditions the legal relationship between citizen and State in some general, overarching manner, or (b) enlarges or diminishes the scope of what we would now regard as fundamental constitutional rights.[3]

---

justified search and seizure of property absent a lawful warrant. Dissimilarly, in Britain, the absence of a written constitution prevents such entrenchment, whereby the most recent will of Parliament can instead terminate or even reverse well-established principles necessary to maintain the rule of law and democratic society. Despite this ever-present risk, the thrust of its concern for the protection of civil liber-ties has remained fundamentally preserved, eloquently captured in the judgment of Camden LJ: 'The great end, for which men entered into society, was to secure their property. That right is preserved sacred and incommunicable in all instances...By the laws of England, every inva-sion of private property, be it ever so minute, is a trespass. No man can set his foot upon my ground without my license.' Duly, the rights of the individual are residual; he is entitled to act in all manners which are not overtly proscribed by law, whereas the State may act only if duly authorized to do so by law.

1 [1934] 1 KB 590

2 *Thoburn v Sunderland City Council* [2003] QB 151

3 Examples of such constitutional statutes likely include the Magna

The integration of the United Kingdom within the European Union further exacerbates the difficulty of any attempt to protect the integrity of the common law, inasmuch EU law is now sovereign over even domestic legislation,[1] by way of the principle of direct effect.[2] This is not to say that EU law likely jeopardizes the rights of individuals; in fact, European legislation generally, especially in the guise of the European Convention on Human Rights, first drafted by the Council of Europe in 1950, arguably enshrines the political and economic liberties of its member-citizens better than the legal code in any single member state party to the treaty. Rather, it is to say that in the absence of domestic provisions which entrench fundamental civic rights, such as via a formal constitution (which the United Kingdom lacks), the risk of their violation increases if only due to the transfer of political authority outside of domestic institutions—in this case, from Westminster to Strasbourg. The closer proximity between such national political bodies and the citizens whose rights they are charged to protect engenders greater transparency and responsiveness to public grievances, rather than the sluggish reaction of distant supranational entities like the EU, often criticized for its 'democratic deficit' and the aloofness that creates as regards sensitive lawmaking appertaining to the lives of hundreds of millions across more than two dozen countries.

International law proper suffers from even worse defects, not least because of the greater heterogeneity of its state membership. The absence of any global legislature or executive renders collaborative efforts binding, due more to custom[3] than to

---

Carta, the Bill of Rights 1689, the Acts of Union 1707, the European Communities Act 1972 and the Human Rights Act 1998. Although such legislation cannot be permanently entrenched, unlike 'ordinary' statutes, they are not subject to implied repeal; any alteration of them must instead be expressly worded to that effect.

1 *Flaminio Costa v ENEL* [1964] ECR 585 (6/64)

2 *Van Gend en Loos v Nederlandse Administratie der Belastingen* (1963) Case 26/62

3 I speak here namely of the chief principle of customary international law, *pacta sunt servanda*—that every international obligation is fulfilled in good faith.

actual enforcement capability (*i.e.*, through the use of force).[1] While there is an international judiciary in the form of the International Court of Justice (itself the primary judicial organ of the United Nations), jurisdiction is based exclusively on the consent of states appearing before it, thereby severely limiting its effectiveness. The lack of any significant supranational military similarly precludes any legal duty incumbent upon states being truly obligatory, if not for frail reciprocal expectations. As discussed, law is inseparable from politics, and nowhere is its infiltration greater than within the international realm. There, geopolitical and transnational economic considerations shape not only the content of legal policy but reduce its efficacy as relied upon by relatively-weaker nations via the double-standard applied against them by stronger ones, themselves often immune from compliance to those obligations which prove inconvenient. A myriad of cases unfortunately illustrate this trend, particularly as concern the jealous regard with which states guard their territorial boundaries and the unfettered discretion to use force in the name of national security, even if contrary to international protocol.

Legal Constitutionalism

While we acknowledge that ethics and law remain distinct sciences, the jurisprudential route best able to furnish consilience between them is found in *legal constitutionalism*, the idea that judges are principally charged with the crafting of law, its content and application. However, the enormous power wielded by such an unelected judicial elite has been likened by critics to a bureaucratized enlightened despotism. They rather retain faith in the political processes of representative democracy, such that elected *politicians*, rather than jurists, should ultimately be afforded unlimited discretion in the formation of laws, while the

---

1 The internationally lawful use of force is confined to exceptional circumstances as defined under Chapter VII of the United Nations Charter.

judiciary is instead presented the humbler task of mere interpretation rather than legislation. Of course, neither system is without flaw, but there are powerful arguments, both principled and pragmatic, why the present political constitutionalism found in Britain should be buttressed by greater judicial supremacy.

Deriving our argument from first principles, the existence of a moral hierarchy of value lends itself to the understanding that certain perspectives are to be provided greater consideration than others by virtue of both the refinement of their views and the breadth of experience which informs them. Common sense dictates that the axiological preferences of juridical scholars, well-versed in the application of law as both a tool of moral inculcation and policymaking, should be given precedence, if not outright supremacy, to the views shared by laymen (politicians amongst them). A knee-jerk counterargument might concern the danger of democratic ideals becoming hijacked by these aloof judges sitting on high, but we must not forget that protection of individual liberties is best safeguarded once taken out of the hands of the mass, not least because the sanctity of legal rights and freedoms must not be conflated with mere majoritarianism. Whereas individual citizens are less concerned with complying with a sociolegal framework in which every man's rights and interests are best preserved, ensuring this delicate balance is the central concern for any judge: that no law can work to the unjustified disadvantage of any sector of society, however feared or prejudiced against by an overwhelming majority, is the preserve of law and order—not populist sentiment. For, if we were to invest all our hopes within a political sphere governed by a simple majority, rather than, in the words of Madison, in those "enlightened statesmen...able to adjust these clashing interests, and render them all subservient to the public good,"[1] imagine how slower the fullest bloom of civilization? How much longer would be retarded the spirit of equality amongst men of all races, between the sexes, amongst the opportunities of health, educa-

---

1 Federalist No. 10, 1787.

tion and employment afforded to every citizen as a matter of right rather than privilege? To have such unwavering faith in the public sphere is to ensure one day its almost certain loss.

Accordingly, a greater investiture of power must be given to the judiciary so as to ensure its independence from both political machination and populist will, thereby guarding against the latter ever proving contrary to notions of either the rule of law or fundamental principles of human flourishing. Absent these excesses, the highest duty of judges is the maximal welfare of the individual as available through legal means, whether as a matter of civic rights or entitlement to access vital social goods. This must remain their responsibility despite even the vociferations of the electorate, or their lack thereof (insofar as many are ignorant or so uninitiated as to express an informed opinion regarding any coherent stance on the very social issues upon which judges are forced to rule). Rarely is the common man spared enough time or motivation to pursue an acquaintance with those matters which turn out to have the gravest impact on his affairs; contemplation of such convoluted topics is ironically the preserve of those often relatively untouched by their effects—that is, the impartial members of a reclusive judiciary. Even more so than elected officials are judges provided the disinterested perspective required in the sensible resolution of quintessentially *political* disputes[1] involving topical social concerns of the day, for the

---

1 That judges are better equipped to resolve private disagreements, whether the complex commercial wrangling of two corporate entities or the custody battle fought between estranged spouses over their children, should go unchallenged in that the handling of such conflicts requires ample legal training so that centuries of accumulated procedural and substantive knowledge may be applied uniformly and fairly. However, the extent of judicial autonomy cannot be unlimited, for the rule of law is intimately connected to its efficacy, which cannot thrive for long outside the realm of fundamental majoritarian support. Therefore, the idea of heightened judicial activism does not necessarily conflict with a constitutional structure in which the legislature is *ultimately* sovereign, whilst still permitting greater oversight of legislation's compliance with the preservation of basic civil and social rights. Under such a system the courts ought to be allowed to preliminarily strike down unconstitutional laws, whereby their disapproval is likely to carry significant moral authority urging the legislature toward re-

goodwill of politicians is suspect insofar as the often conflicting aims of popularity *vis-à-vis* re-election and serving the best interests of the populace. That a judge must concern himself with neither such distracting factors as likeability nor public image is a blessing which facilitates a unique opportunity to concentrate on the most germane aspects of any case, permitting a clarity of judgment largely absent from those embroiled in the biased infighting endemic to any controversial issue—politicians chief among them. Such clarity affords not only freedom from the slavish representation of constituents, which can predictably cancel itself out between those elected by rivaling groups, but permits a perspicuity which refrains from treating any political issue in isolation from relevant others and at the same time lends foresight into the ramifications of how a given judgment may shape the decision of future cases.

Such is the majesty of the law, uniquely equipped to ensure the stable resolution of conflicting interests at their most basic level—whether between citizen and State in public matters or citizen and citizen in private ones—and to thereupon inform social values so as to promote the public morality, refined and codified in established law, carrying with it the inertia of precedent. The ethics it espouses is neither heroic nor corrupt, but a minimal baseline, a creeping yardstick against which is slowly improved the generic moral fiber of the common man through the progressive reshaping of those legal standards to which he is expected to adhere. The glory of this undertaking is not to be underestimated, for every attempt to further secure the rights of men is to contrive a fiction; there are no rights cast in the cosmos, but only those utile rules born by the will and sagacity of law. Whereas social progress is relentless, accelerated in equal but opposite parts by the fearless march of technology on one hand and an ever-expanding social conscience on the other, law

---

form; however, ultimate popular will may be preserved if the judicial nullification is capable of being overridden by a subsequent legislative veto, an act whose gravity should likely require a super-majority.

serves as the conservative institution waiting to adjudicate on the soundest means forward, incrementally regulating those social and scientific innovations which ensure individual and collective prosperity. Whereupon this cautious balancing act, admittedly of an essentially political nature, is split apart from judicial conscience, thus ends the rule of law; and society, however democratic, becomes governed by mob-rule, for there is no buffer to refine the cacophonous, uncoordinated demands of the great multitude.

    —M.D. Levenstein

    Cambridge, England

    August 2013

PART I: MAXIMS

INTRODUCTION: THE IMPRINT OF EQUITY

THE GENIUS OF EQUITY as a curative to the unyielding rigors of the common law is one of the great legal triumphs of the past millennium. Since the reign of Richard II, the Court of Chancery, administered by the Lord Chancellor, was developed as its own separate legal organ. This was distinct from the courts of yore which had previously been governed by the fickleness of the "King's Conscience" and became characterized by a more congealed set of principled guidelines. Whilst originally confined to trusts of land and management of the estates of lunatics and minors, this once nascent and inconspicuous appendage of legal thought has since bourgeoned into one of the predominant intellectual forces underpinning modern civil law. This transformation has never been more clearly witnessed than in the historic Judicature Acts of the 1870s.[1]

---

1 The Judicature Act of 1873 (ss. 3, 4) abolished the traditional distinction between the Courts of Chancery, Common Pleas, Queen's Bench and Exchequer, amongst others, consolidating them into the newly-created Supreme Court of Judicature. More importantly, the Act sought to streamline the divergent legal outcomes generated by separate courts of law and equity, such that remedies afforded by both were now available under a scheme unified not only in substance but pleading and procedure. Not only did this reduce the jurisdictional arbitrage endemic amongst litigants who would seek the most favorable

Heavily influenced by the precepts of natural law, equity is chiefly occupied by concerns of conscience—that is, matters invoking fairness and equitable dealing. One of the primary drivers which expanded its jurisdiction entailed the long-standing deficiencies of the common law writ system, which insisted that unless a preexisting writ was issued for a fee, no legitimate cause of action would permit the matter to be heard before the Royal Courts. The Court of Chancery steadily accreted the purview to hear such disputes as a matter of course instead of the sovereign himself, who, swamped by petitions, was unable to personally carry out so onerous a task. Equity adopted a more flexible approach toward the resolution of legal disputes, many of which had yet to be formally classified but whose novelty would not bar them from due consideration—unlike under the former writ system. Ironically, fusion with the common law as practiced by the courts required uniformity, such that by the 19ᵗʰ century, equity had evolved into as technical and rule-bound a discipline as the common law it first sought to ameliorate.

Of course, the imprint of equity did not dissolve with the passage of time; rather, its influence remains so robust that many legal commentators question the need for any ongoing distinction between itself and its common law counterpart, as opposed to a system which universalized equitable principles. There is much traction in this position, especially as concerns the unfortunate limitations imposed on enforcing equitable maxims via relatively-impoverished common law procedures and available remedies. No doubt the critical reception of the common law is strongly colored by viewing equity as the fullest realization of the jurisprudential grounding of law itself: the practicable manifestation of moral philosophy within society. This is the ultimate ambition of equity: the fusion of the ethical with the legal. Never has this amalgamation between wholly

---

outcome depending on whether the court hearing the dispute would apply the rules of the common law or equity, but where the two sets of rules conflicted, equity would come to prevail.

complete in any legal system, owing as much to administrative unviability as competing conceptions of the Good. Nonetheless, this is equity's surreptitious goal, and one remarkably successful throughout its historical infiltration of much judge-made law, particularly as relates to land, tort and contract.

Too often, the study of law suffers from one of two unfortunate maladies; either firstly, the removal of its relevance from daily life—that is, the abstraction of legal principle from advice concerning its tangible consequences in the lives of litigants— or secondly, the unquestioned acknowledgement of the soundness of its moral foundations. As the former is best addressed via practical demonstration, it should be of little surprise that our present medium best lends itself to an exploration of the latter defect. We shall examine the philosophical—in particular ethical—and practical legitimacy of not only the maxims which govern the application of equity, but also the remedies available to realize their potential. Our focus shall remain within the English system, but the vast majority of what is to be observed will be germane to any common law jurisdiction. One of the great strengths of equity is its flexibility toward resolving the irreducibly complex and contested affairs of daily life, none of which could ever be perfectly anticipated in advance. Of course, this fluidity brings with it a rare intellectual challenge, and one intensified by our understanding that equity is circumscribed not only externally by the common law, but too internally by its conflicting aims of achieving justice whilst at times being straitjacketed by the rigidity of its own rules—namely, the clash between looking to intent rather than form.

A Legacy of Trust

Equity, with its superb grasp of human motivation and intention, is uniquely situated to impartially take up the gauntlet where disputes arise regarding private ownership and the rights exercisable thereon. Nowhere has its contribution been more profound than with the trust of land—a brilliant piece of conveyancing machinery which bifurcates ownership between the nominal legal titleholder and the true recipient of its fruits, the beneficiary. At first blush, this may appear to be a strictly dry and amoral undertaking, but, in fact, this device operates to provide the legal means for placing a premium upon the autonomy of the individual. By capturing the specific, oftentimes convoluted, intentions of parties,[1] equity law is able to entwine the piercing insights of psychology with the tangible manifestation of binding proprietary entitlement to craft a scenario in which the benefits of earned labor are distributed not only as per the wishes of their bearer (the settlor), but also so as to maximize their utility, both amongst the widest class of beneficiaries and per the utmost standards of enlightened management. Again, not only is equity able to furnish the legal facilitation of charity (through the trust of property itself for the benefit of beneficiaries, or, say, a gratuitous gift), but also the assurance of meting out the just due of parties where breaches of trust occur (*e.g.*, requiring the trustee to personally compensate the beneficiary for an unauthorized or irresponsible loss).

These multiple objectives are achieved by the complex breadth of functions performed by the modern trust. So long as the fundamental constituent elements are in place to include a trustee, a beneficiary, and the fiduciary duty owed by the former to the latter, we have at first blush the makings of a valid trust. Of course, this relationship must be differentiated from what it is *not*, such as a gift, bailment, any principal-agent scenario or contract (including debts). While some of these arrangements may have characteristics of trusts, each, to varying extents, lacks the

---

1 This difficulty is aided insofar as the 'three certainties' must first be satisfied before the existence of a valid trust: *certainty of intention* (on the part of the settlor to specifically create a trust), *certainty of subject matter* (as regards the intended trust property) and *certainty of objects* (unambiguous identity of the beneficiaries, except in the case of charitable trusts). Moreover, equity is uniquely competent to deal with the potential difficulties which arise upon the subsequent variation of trusts, both statutorily (the Variation of Trusts Act 1958) and through precedent (the rule in *Saunders v Vautier* [1841]).

essential cleavage between legal and beneficial ownership. Contracts further require consideration (unnecessary in the enforcement of a valid trust),[1] whereas gifts transfer property without the imposition of conditions. Trusts are further subdivided by form and function, most broadly by type of beneficiary, whether named persons or defined purpose. Whereas the latter is generally only valid if of a charitable design, the former is more varied structurally, taking shape despite fluctuating degrees of clarity (from *express* at its most unambiguous to *implied* by operation of law in predetermined circumstances). Express trusts, by virtue of their greater articulation, encompass a wide gamut of species, including fixed and discretionary (relating to trustee duties), secret or half-secret (relating to public disclosure of trust terms by testamentary disposition) and protective trusts and superannuation schemes (relating to the prescient investment of funds for the benefit of either profligate or numerous beneficiaries, respectively). While each of the aforesaid types of trust shares much in common, this simplified classification merely serves to partly pinpoint the bases for their qualitative differentiation. This oftentimes unnoticed multiplicity of effects, both legal and philosophical, is perfected in the trust, which establishes a relationship between the trustee and beneficiary of duties, and vice versa as one of rights. Of course, the impact of equity is multifarious, including also the domain of restrictive covenants, estoppel (both proprietary and promissory), the mortgagor's equitable right of redemption and even the subpoena. Let us take each one briefly in turn.

Covenants are promises recognized by law which, unlike contractual bargains, are so solemn in their undertaking that they may be absent of consideration if properly sealed. Like trusts, their recognition in equity speaks to the paramount respect for personal autonomy granted by this branch of law, but

---

1 Despite this general difference, the mere presence of a contract does not necessarily preclude the existence of a trust: *Barclays Bank Ltd v Quitclose Investments Ltd* (1970).

to an extent no further than as agreed upon by consenting parties—that is to say, an agreement which does not unduly bind third parties with potentially operose burdens.[1] Thus, as regards freehold covenants regulating the usage of land, only those restrictive in nature are recognized in equity and may bind successive purchasers.

Estoppel is a fundamental doctrine of equity, essentially allowing the relaxation of strict legal right in any situation where its exercise would yield injustice. Most often, this concerns an attempt by one party to renege on a promise upon which the other party has innocently relied, thereby incurring a detriment. Equity recognizes that estoppel can be either promissory (relating to *any* inequitable result pursuant to the promisor failing to keep his word which was preceded by the promisee's change of position)[2] or proprietary (relating to present or future representations regarding entitlement to land incurring detrimental reliance). Notably, whereas the former is only a defense, the latter may be invoked as a cause of action.

Next we have the all-important mortgagor's right to redeem. Originally found at common law, whereupon the homeowner mortgaged his land as security, if he failed to discharge his debt by the date listed in his mortgage contract, he would lose *all* rights over his property. Equity sought to correct this injustice by permitting repayment of the loan subsequent to the redemp-

---

1 *Rhone v Stephens* [1994] 2 AC 310. Per the judgment of Lord Templeman, 'Equity cannot compel an owner to comply with a positive covenant entered into by his predecessors...Enforcement of a positive covenant lies in contract...To enforce a positive covenant would be to enforce a personal obligation against a person who has not covenanted.' Of course, the *benefit* of a covenant may be transmitted without difficulty to a third party, per the Contracts (Rights of Third Parties) Act 1999.
2 The doctrine of promissory estoppel was controversially resurrected by Lord Denning in *Central London Property Trust Ltd v High Trees House Ltd* (1947), following its debut in *Hughes v Metropolitan Railway Co.* (1877). As it is discretionary, it is difficult to envisage reliance upon estoppel in the absence of detriment (although this is not strictly necessary), not so much for reasons of principle (*i.e.* a promise should be binding regardless of detriment), but the broader policy considerations of limiting litigation if otherwise available for non-consequentialist outcomes (*e.g.* where there is no actual harm or miscarriage of justice).

tion date, as well as minimizing the availability of foreclosure, whereupon the failure to repay the mortgage debt still permitted the homeowner to preserve his financial security insofar as the extent to which he had, at the time of default, paid off his mortgage. This is an acutely vivid instance of the intervention of equity in alleviating the harsh procedures which once depleted the mortgagor's entire proprietary entitlement.

Lastly, we shall touch upon the writ of subpoena, originally devised by John de Waltham, Bishop of Salisbury, under the reign of Richard II, as a court order issued by the Court of Chancery initially to compel attendance by the defendant in responding to allegations made by the plaintiff, and later designed to summon witnesses under penalty of contempt. Although today an indispensable fixture of legal proceedings, the force of compelling testimony, either *in personam* (*ad testificandum*) or via the supply of documents (*duces tecum*), so as to permit the defendant to confront his accusers proved a pivotal innovation toward the assurance of a fair trial, and once more, this very *equitable* contribution is not to go overlooked.

Another feature which demarcates the trust as a unique equitable construct is the extensive and onerous set of duties placed upon the trustee in his role as fiduciary. Perhaps most striking is the trustee's inability to dispose of trust assets as he wishes, despite his legal entitlement to do so. Breach of this prohibition may render him personally liable, in addition to any number of actions which a court may characterize as against the best interests of the settlor and/or beneficiary, including a grayscale of questionable moral, if not technically illegal, behaviors, such as acting in bad faith or evincing disloyalty. In this sense, the trustee—a legal position of trust bound by conscience—is the ultimate amalgam of law and ethics, where moral responsibility becomes legally enforceable, not least because the full array of duties incumbent in fair dealing is not capable of exhaustive enumeration in a trust—or any legal—document. The premium placed upon good character in the position of trustee is obliquely signaled by the extensive measures in place to replace him following a breach of any one of his duties, including sections 36 and 41 of the Trustee Act 1925, the latter per the court's statutory jurisdiction to appoint a replacement. This has since been augmented by sections 19-21 of the Trusts of Land and Appointment of Trustees Act 1996 (TLATA), whereby beneficiaries *sui juris* may direct the High Court, per its inherent jurisdiction to manage the affairs of a trust, to remove a trustee and appoint a successor. This is a remarkably far-ranging power, especially in light of *Letterstedt v Broers* (1884), where the beneficiary's application to remove a trustee was successful despite allegations of misconduct on the latter's part (which ultimately proved unfounded). The court decided there were sufficient grounds to replace a trustee even if he produced disharmony (*sans* actual financial loss) amongst the beneficiaries in his administration of the trust. This discretion only magnifies the burden placed upon trustees, whose general fiduciary duties to place the best interests of beneficiaries as their foremost concern also include prohibitions on self-dealing (*Campbell v Walker* [1800]), insider dealing (*Tito v Waddell [No. 2]* [1977]), a general bar on the trustee from charging for his labors (*Barrett v Hartley* [1866]) and of course, the utmost diligence in responsibly investing trust funds. It comes as no surprise, therefore, that the position of fiduciary requires the highest standard of care found in either common law or at equity.

The Value of a Promise

Why keeping one's word is important seems a question falling more within the legal purview of contract than within equity. However, while this is superficially true, we cannot disregard the universal, interdisciplinary legal potency of the idea of a promise, however formulated. In equity, both intention and representation are considered in the dealings with others so as to provide legal recourse in the event of default of said promise. This is most visible in the form of estoppel, which prevents X from escaping the demands of conscience even to the point of barring him from insisting on his strict legal rights against Y, when Y has changed his position as a result of X's specious assurances. Therefore, whereas in contract the concept of a promise is one of *bargain*—a mutually-utile exchange—in equity, the subtler emphasis placed is less utilitarian and, perhaps unwittingly, concerned foremost with the deontic principle of honoring the agreement itself. The high-water mark of this approach was set by Lord Denning in *WJ Alan v El Nasr Export* (1972), where he argued that *detrimental* reliance was not essential to the success of promissory estoppel, though it nevertheless remained a "shield and not a sword" (per his earlier judgment in *Combe v Combe* [1951]). This approach has since met with mixed judicial response.[1]

Accordingly, let us examine the theoretical rigor of this position. Utility as legitimate preference satisfaction is a sensible foundation for the binding quality of any promise, particularly ones involving the explicit exchange of goods and services. To this extent, we may find the notion of detriment as a result of failure to comply with one's commitment obvious. However, does it arise in the "purely" promissory case? Speaking extralegally for a moment, we may find such an example in the case of a pledge of marital fidelity. Imagine the husband, H, vows at the altar to forsake all others sexually for the presumed benefit of his wife, W. Let us further suppose that H is a good provider, a man sensitive to his wife's feelings, and a devoted father to their children. He cares for his wife both sincerely and in every meaningful tangible guise. However, after twenty years of marriage, excitement has long since been replaced by familiarity, and he is given the opportunity to have a one-time and wholly clandestine, emotionally-vapid but physically exciting, rendezvous with a beautiful woman. From a purely utilitarian viewpoint, this is

---

1 Doubt was cast on this view in *Fontana NV v Mautner* (1979), where Balcombe J reasserted the necessity of detriment, following the Privy Council ruling in *Ajayi v RT Briscoe (Nigeria) Ltd* (1964).

hardly objectionable, especially if W never finds out about this liaison, and it brings H pleasure, however temporary. Nevertheless, our moral intuitions, often far more insightful than the most convoluted philosophic argument (and hence a view correctly entertained by the Legal Realists), tell us that such is scarcely innocuous conduct on the part of H. But *why?*—for it is our hapless fate that we cannot believe a thing, however apparent in the heart, unless justifiable to the mind.

Preliminarily assuming this instinct to be of merit, we may further venture to corroborate it by claiming that H's conduct is not inoffensive because he has violated any tangible utile promise (*e.g.,* to ensure that his wife is economically cared for), but rather because he has *devalued the security of the compulsive nature of the promise itself.* This is to say that a breach of a symbolic promise (symbolic insofar as, in our case, the marital infidelity will never be discovered by W, and hence will not be a source of emotional pain for her) is nonetheless damaging, because it intentionally violates the *status quo ante* of just desert between two or more parties. This is best clarified at first instance by reversing roles, so that the idea may be more forcefully and empathetically understood. If H, who had never been unfaithful to W, were told by a third party to *imagine* that his W had been unfaithful, though he never could have reasonable proof of such, and then queried as to whether this upset him, the answer would almost certainly be in the affirmative. When probed, H would likely explain that W's conduct, even if of no direct harmful effect, nonetheless constituted a betrayal which no longer entitled her to H's maintaining *his* promise not to be unfaithful. Therefore, the crux of the matter has little to do with utile gain/loss (though of course one can elaborately characterize the loss of security as negative utility in emotional form), and everything to do with deserving the security of a promise—that is, to not be made *unworthy* of another's conduct, as opposed to positively *punished* for violating the expectations relied upon by another. This difference, though subtle, is illuminating as regards the importance of a promise as recognized by equity. Whereas tangible utile loss is of concern to contracts activated by consideration, the mere failure to recognize a promise may trigger the intervention of equity, again, not because of any net utile loss, but because one party does not deserve the security offered by the certainty of the other's compliance to the same covenant.

To this extent, Lord Denning's ruling regarding the optionality of detriment, as opposed to mere change in position (admittedly taken to an extreme in our case insofar as breaking a promise constitutes a change in circumstances), in *WJ Alan* proves remarkably powerful as a moral statement recognizing this important nuance, though one which has not unexpectedly prompted a cold reception owing to its "victimless" nature. This tension between the deontological and consequentialist is particularly pronounced in equity, that branch of law most concerned with the thoughtful resolution of this debate, and one to which we shall repeatedly aspire toward resolving throughout this text. Unsurprisingly, whereas its foremost original concern was with the strict adherence to matters of principle, its subsequent expansion, complication and congealment have heavily colored its prescriptions with more practical, policy-oriented considerations. Whether this is a welcome trend remains to be assessed.

Where There Is a Will

The arsenal of remedies available under common law has historically been stiflingly confined—namely, monetary damages. Of course, imaginative equity has fashioned a more expansive armory to include specific performance, injunctions, rescission (permitting the unilateral revocation of a contract), rectification (the actual rewriting of the terms of a contract to conform to the parties' improperly-recorded intentions) and the appointment of a receiver to collect revenue from a commercial enterprise subsequent to a mortgage default. These remedies, unlike the right to damages under common law, are accessible only per the discretion of the court, usually where financial compensation is deemed inadequate to right the wrong in question. However, under the Senior Courts Act 1981, financial recompense (in the guise of damages) may exist alongside the issuance of either specific performance or injunction. What is chiefly pronounced here is unwillingness on the part of equity to permit pedantic formality, insofar as it is capable of looking to the parties' actual intentions. Equally, there exists an inbuilt legal creativity designed so as not to limit the reservoir of options available to litigants in evenhandedly and effectively resolving their disputes.

The general principles which guide courts toward the application of the aforementioned remedies are numerous, and each shall be expounded both in light of its legal efficacy and, as is less critically assessed, its philosophical tractability as a moral rule—of especial concern to us, considering the primacy placed by equity upon *doing* good, as opposed to merely facilitating its eventuation.[1] Oftentimes, this conflict is staged not only on the battleground of competing conceptions of moral priority—such as macroscopic considerations of logistical efficiency versus idiographic fair treatment (the canonical "certainty versus justice" debate)—but also in light of ample ambiguity regarding the intentions of the settlor, especially subsequent to his death. In this sense, equity is both a blind and half-deaf Justice, unable to hear as intelligibly the calls of her most relevant petitioner, the clarity of whose wishes have been mutilated to the point of risking arbitrary third-party reinterpretation. No doubt, much of the task of equity is akin to escaping a labyrinth, hardly a matter of simple extrication.

---

1 Perhaps this uncommonly lofty legal aspiration is no better realized than in the guise of the cy-près doctrine, which aids the court to give effect to a charitable trust whenever its preconceived intention cannot be precisely executed, but whereupon the courts, by virtue of their inherent jurisdiction, are reluctant to allow the trust to fail for lack of approximating its original purpose.

Chapter I: *Lex Naturalis*

NOTWITHSTANDING THE OSSIFICATION which has over centuries encrusted equity and transformed it from a discipline once indistinguishable from the governance of man's (albeit necessarily flawed) conscience to one now, for all its purported flexibility, marked by rigid doctrinarism and technicality, equity remains the last and best bastion appealing to the highest moral principles which hold aloft our corpus of law. As Bracton had already observed by the mid-13th century, equity was essentially the bespoke realization of justice between the specified parties in question, rather than the application of Aristotelian distributive justice as found at common law. Such an approach was in stark contrast to the precedence-laden common law famously challenged by Sir Francis Bacon, then Attorney General, in his opinion in the *Earl of Oxford's Case* (1616), reaffirming the position as formerly articulated by Lord Ellesmere that the chancery courts maintained the authority to override common law rulings.

The constellation of ethical precepts which steers the court toward an equitable outcome is unsurprisingly vague in its original formulation, despite ample historical evidence of how such principles ought to be practicably applied in legal disputes. There is no exact number of maxims of equity, for depending upon the interpreter, some may be fused with others, or disregarded altogether. In this text, because we are specifically interested in the jurisprudence of the axioms of equity, a scrupulously conservative position has been taken so as to include all possible candidates, thus rendering our number eighteen. The maxims herein examined have been categorized by function; the first class appeals to principles of natural law, the second to procedural formality and efficiency, while the final class is a loosely-related collection of doctrines preoccupied with aiding the court in settling tangential or preliminary considerations before turning to the graver task of addressing the crux of the given legal matter.

We first turn to those maxims derived from *lex naturalis*, for the perceived transcendent universality of the moral force of its edicts has historically been the foremost intellectual justification for the supremacy of not only equity but also statutory law, in English jurisprudence. This ancient predisposition is first recorded in the works of Bracton and later Fortescue, the former of whom referred to equity as appealing to the "fountainhead of justice from which all rights derive,"[1] that fountainhead being God-given reason. Fortescue adopts Bracton's endorsement of Italian natural law jurists such as Bassianus and his pupil, Azo of Bologna, though with a sterner emphasis on inculcating virtue within society through authoritarian guidelines rather than a juridical culture which encouraged reflectiveness on the part of the citizenry. Nonetheless, such writers were the shoulders upon which Sir Edward Coke's legal genius stood, he who served as the preeminent proponent of natural law of his era. As he wrote in *Calvin's Case* (1608): "The law of nature is that which God infused into man's heart...our allegiance is due unto the law of nature before any judicial or municipal law: [it] is immutable." It is fitting, therefore, that we begin with the most conspicuous

---

1 *De Legibus et Consuetudinibus Angliae*, circa 1235.

tradition of the moral justification of equitable doctrine in English jurisprudence.

Substance Over Form

Basic though it may appear, this maxim is the prerequisite not only to all others concerning equity's relationship to natural law, but too the very uniqueness of this legal discipline. Law is a subject riven with the schizophrenic malady of attempting to pacify the evils of men whilst imposing the magnified errs of its very architects. This necessarily, and perhaps more problematically, occurs on a substantive level, but it may be a more readily mendable defect as regards form. By form is intended procedure—those niggling rules whose purpose is not the maintenance of justice but the assurance of expedience. Ranging from statutes of limitation to rules on admissible evidence to even blanket proscriptions on rendering decisions curtailing national policy, we find in equity this clash most prominent between legal and beneficial entitlement. No doubt equity is occasionally trapped by its own ingenuity, unable to rectify every abuse of position and thereby unwittingly rewarding breach of fiduciary duty, particularly as regards vulnerable beneficiaries whose very susceptible nature first spurred misguided faith on the part on the settlor in the trustee(s). Nonetheless, as a matter of principle, equity seeks to combat this unfortunate risk through the aforesaid maxim: that substance, especially as manifested by the intention of the parties in question, shall trump mere formality.

The most illuminating case on point is *Paul v Constance* (1977), where the personal injury compensation received by H, and orally promised to his *de facto* partner (despite his still being married to his estranged wife, W), was sufficient to trigger a trust in his partner's—the plaintiff's—favor for a one-half share, following H dying intestate. The Court of Appeal clarified what would establish the first of the three certainties (the certainty of intention), and brought effect to the aforesaid maxim in ruling that a settlor's "*words* [emphasis added]...show a clear intention to dispose of property...so that someone else acquires a beneficial interest."[1] Of course, there are circumscriptions placed upon even so liberal an interpretation as this, and ones carefully delineated in the seminal case of *Jones v Lock* (1865). Here, Lord Cranworth LC issued the judgment in the Court of Appeal in Chancery to correctly draw the line insofar that the absence of any intention to establish a trust could not permit the court to create one, despite this meaning that an intended, albeit imperfectly construed, gift, must fail. *Jones v Lock* provides clear evidence of another equitable maxim, that is, the reluctance to perfect an imperfect gift for want of proper formality, not least because in the case of gifts, the outright and gratuitous transfer of property must be treated with greater caution.

What of the freestanding sensibility of this maxim? Is the "substance over form" rule justified independently of legal reasons? Perhaps a more tractable approach to addressing this otherwise hopelessly open-ended question is to pose it in reverse: should form *ever* trump substance? While our intuition might direct a negative response, meaningful insight is rarely the fruit of spontaneity. Preliminarily, assuming the law to be an ennobling undertaking precisely because it stakes normative claims—that is, it posits an objective axiology which prioritizes certain ends over others—rather than one devoid of any value hierarchy, it follows that the law must ultimately and fundamentally be concerned with the moral content of parties' decisions and their consequences, as opposed to the relatively banal consideration of the specific form in which they are manifested. Of course, this is not an uncontroversial assumption. Despite the inertia of jurisprudential scholars regarding the law as a principally substantive discipline, positivists generally, including such notable figures as Hart and Raz, have powerfully argued that law as a means of social control may be readily divorced from any underlying meta-ethical interests. While this is not the view endorsed here, it would be seemingly meaningless to speak of the law without

1 [1977] 1 WLR 527 (CA)

some appeal to the self-contained procedures it employs to lend legitimacy firstly to its edicts (most visibly by approval through the due legislative process) and subsequently to their successful implementation (via effective sanctioning for their breach, such as through the threat of punishment by the state), for without them, we are left with an impotent philosopher-king ruling over his unenlightened people—and without the benefit of a police force. Therefore, whereas both a substantive and positive view appear necessary on a conceptual level, where exactly the balance should be struck is less clear.

Notwithstanding such imprecision as regards the proper focus of our discipline, substantive justice must always be the foremost concern of legal practitioners, for the alternative, purely positivist conception of legal rules as being devoid of action-guiding content permits a system which could be transplanted without regard for culture, history or societal norms beyond solely administrative traditions. To disconnect law in this way from both the body politic and organic society is as disastrous as it is futile. There can be no law absent values by whose criteria it is legitimized, and whereupon such values must therefore be upheld. This of course lends itself to further inquiry, such as, who is and ought to be responsible for axiological determinations? The legal formalists insist it ought to be the legislature, whereas the instrumentalists insist that legal interpretative creativity only meaningfully exists within the purview of an interventionist judicial elite. As with so many misguided academic debates, a viable—and sound—solution is not to be found in either extreme; however, the extent of justifying legal formalism extends no further than that of the democratic mandate, itself a suspicious premise insofar as the public's lacked interest and expertise in the diligent creation of law hardly renders them qualified to serve as its final source of approval. Thus, that the public should ultimately be the overriding check upon legal norms is sensible if for no reason other than its being realistically necessary so as to neutralize social unrest. In spite of this provision only being relevant following the most egregious instances of the abuse of legislative and, necessarily, political power, it nonetheless serves as an exception to the rule which instead confers upon a judicial elite the charge of authoritatively interpreting law so as not only to nimbly tailor its remedies for the assistance of those given parties to a dispute but also to ever-reflect upon the precedential implications of their judgments as is required in a common law system.

Duly, judicial supremacy is defensible not only because those intimately involved in any proceeding have the sufficient insight to provide effective solutions, and whereby the proximate and impartial office of a judge is therefore best situated to fulfill this role rather than some distant legislator, but more pressingly, that the law as a science is not to be left wholly unattended in the hands of those "lawmakers" who are so often woefully undereducated in its curriculum. That merit, and not mass appeal, must be the criterion which is prized in legal assessment respects the premium to be placed upon the quality of individual judicial scholarship rather than populist appeasement, the latter of which can all too often come at the expense of achieving justice, especially where minority rights are concerned. Such should be of little surprise to those who so stingingly realize that prudence has never been the preserve of popularity, and that sagacity is necessarily a rarity. We may tentatively conclude that the substance of good law is had within the domain of the judges, whereas the veneer of formal legitimacy is rendered in any democratic state by the legislature, whereupon the starkest danger of such formality exists in the realm of procedural efficiency as epitomized in statutory, rather than common, law. Certainty at the expense of justice has never been a comfortable pathway for jurists to follow, not least because of their proximity to the conflict in question; however, so as to permit the bureaucratic mechanisms of justice to function smoothly (or as smoothly as is possible, barring the danger of overburdened collapse), it remains a practical necessity in light of the voluminous backlog of cases which ever threatens to overwhelm our courts. An impervious constitutional argument, if not a principled one, cauterizing this debate is the acceptance of the hitherto ultimate political fact: the sovereignty of Parliament.

Our analysis of this maxim, however, is inseparable not from the auspices of political or logistical reality, but rather *equity*—which must hold itself above the tawdry undertakings of practicable calculation *if, and only if,* to do so would come at the expense of its mandate: to ensure justice between the parties. Accordingly, the rule is sound insofar as substance, when readily corroborated by appropriate evidence and whose exclusion would prevent an equitable outcome for the meritorious party, must always trump the mere pedantry of form. The hobgoblins of technicality which vex the unimaginative pose only a danger once they adversely encumber the fair due of others, at which point their small-mindedness threatens practical justice. Too often the danger of justice understood only literally is forgotten, as with despotic Temures, who vowed to the warriors of Sebastia not to shed their blood upon surrender. They capitulated, and he buried them alive. Let it not be said he was not a man of his word. The power of substantive justice being the only genuine kind therefore leads us naturally to our next, and perhaps most singularly important, equitable maxim: that for every wrong there is a remedy.

To Right Every Wrong

All law, no matter its content or era, is flawed, because man is flawed. Equity could not plausibly surmount this very *human* limitation, but its charge is nevertheless to attempt the impossible. Of course, a central wrinkle which appears in the fabric of equity is its inability to fully transcend the *legal* so as to enter the realm of the strictly moral. That is to say, the limits of equity are the outer limits of the normative ethical content of existing law. Equity can only go so far in extending the grasp of judicial dispute resolution with moral creativity, which accordingly forces its remedies to principally target distinct legal, as opposed to amorphously-defined (however compelling) moral, wrongs.

As was lamentably noted by Mann J in *Dubey v Revenue and Customs Commissioners* (2006), in light of the defect in a declaration of trust amongst other obstacles, some of which were arguably nothing more than trifling technicalities, his hands were nevertheless tied when prompted to provide relief on the part of the applicant administrators of a Christmas savings scheme whose customers, mostly from low-income families, were denied both compensation for the otherwise lost money paid into the scheme and the Christmas food and presents for which they had paid. Despite equity's best intentions, this case vividly reminds us that its remedies are designed only to rectify unconscionable behaviors as recognized at law and not the court of public opinion. However, this important exception aside, we must further unpack what is perhaps equity's most famous maxim.

While not to be taken literally, its thrust conveys that equity, whilst admittedly constrained, is nevertheless more flexible than other areas of law to fashion remedies in response to immoral behavior *so long as it is in the context of a legally-unauthorized* undertaking. This is not an empty statement, for it is impossible to define with any precision the wide gamut of unacceptable breaches of moral duty, such that upon any one of them, so long as coincident with a breach of legal responsibility, compensation can be calculated taking the moral—and not solely legal—opprobrium into account. Equity must therefore delimit its moral ambitions to preexisting breaches of law, though taking into account the scale of a defendant's extralegal wrongfulness. For instance, the punishment exacted upon a trustee in breach of his fiduciary duty is measured by the extent of his *immoral* gain (usually coincident with the magnitude of his ill-gotten economic profit) and general disloyalty, not only with reference to the welfare of the beneficiary, but too the wishes of the settlor. Equity fashions respect for the uniqueness of every wrong, not predominantly in the traditional guise of common law damages (only the most reprehensible or calculated of which incur punitive damages), but rather in the broader range of its afforded remedies. *Quia timet* injunctions are a prime example indicating that the chief purpose behind the flexibility of equitable remedies is to avoid the suffering of wrongs, even to the point of their prevention rather than subsequent compensation. No similar remedy designed to prevent anticipated infringement of the rights of a claimant is found under common law, whose focus is instead on reparation after such misconduct. Of course, equity has devised a much wider range of novel solutions, including not only several other types of injunction, but account of profits, rescission, rectification, restitution and specific performance. These are not always available, however, following the prudent guidelines set forth in *Shelfer v City of London Electric Lighting Co Ltd* (1895), where the rule emerged that in certain circumstances, damages might be more appropriate. The conditions laid down included that where the loss to the claimant was a) small, b) adequately compensable in purely monetary terms and where c) the otherwise imposition of an injunction would be unnecessarily oppressive, damages would be awarded instead.

The bounded ambit of equity's ambition is well-justified, lest we fail to remember that law is not synonymous with moral philosophy. However, we are not concerned with the descriptive here, but its troublesome cousin, the prescriptive. For what is the value of law if not its appeal to the objectively Good? Neither moral nihilists nor relativists can subscribe to such an argument, for replete within its premises is the assertion that there is a distinct moral order which may be elucidated. And, considering the array of potential candidates for the Good which the law may seek to uphold, it appears most sensible to find recourse in the conclusions of liberal political philosophy—that it is reasoned discourse in the public sphere of ideas, rather than appeal to the vagaries of emotivism, which contains the means by which we may separate the wheat from the chaff.

It is not the goal of this work to supply an independent ethical framework; I have allowed my imagination to run sufficiently wild in this regard in preceding works. Accordingly, our attempts to supply the law with an objective moral skeleton will be modest and brief. The first—and as herein argued, indisputable—criterion of legitimate law is the pursuit of justice. Justice is the attainment of hedonic reciprocity between parties, alike in both magnitude and (as far as is detectable) intention. The main function of law is maintaining social order, and, in its sporadic collapse, to issue authoritative resolutions which bind the parties under threat of both economic and penal sanction. Beyond this strict functionalist understanding, there is an unambiguous threshold which must be crossed in order to supply to the law its substantive value. The key requirement which must be satisfied is the just resolution of disputes. Society is an organic agglutination of individuals, each of whom would be essentially deprived of the fruits of civilized existence if not for their respective faith in the freedom of non-exploitative interdependence. Law as justice is the simplest means of ensuring that this prerequisite of social order is ensured, in the commercial sphere by promoting transactions of fundamentally equivalent utile value and in the criminal sphere by meting out punishments for offences proportionate to the scale by which they deprive others of the effective exercise of their rights.

We could, without difficulty, furnish a litany of further attributes of good law, such as the binding recognition of charitable acts and the framework in which prioritization of conflicting aims between the interests of the individual and the collective is possible. However, such would overstep the mark of this book, and thus we confine our focus to the establishment of justice—that value essential in the orderly performance of our daily tasks, whether professional or avocational, quotidian or exceptional. For without faith in the impartial enforcement of our just due, the merit behind the idea of voluntary interdependent association crumbles—the very idea of the necessity of society collapses. The prevention of this calamity must be the highest duty of law.

If so, then what does this say for those instances where the law, and particularly equity, cannot furnish a just solution, morally speaking, because of the limiting factor of legal trip-wires? This poses a serious problem, but not owing to the contestability of those moral values sought to be upheld by the law (for we have already noted the universal appeal—both in philosophic and practical terms—of justice as such an undisputed moral end). Instead, the issue concerned is the defensibility of permitting an unequivocal moral, albeit not legal, wrong to go unremedied. I can find no principled basis for this position, especially in light of the inevitable yet inadequate response that such flexibility would render our system of justice inundated with cases of the bizarre and frivolous; for if we, as jurists, are to take seriously our solemn oath to uphold the nobility of the law, the mere inexpedience of its application should pose no threat to our charge. If so, then a man's right to have his case heard in court should be subject to the proviso that the docket must not be flooded during that particular calendar term, or that the right to appeal should be denied if only because its absence renders a far less time-consuming legal process. Such cannot be the foundations for our system of justice; such is why we would rather let free a dozen guilty men than wrongly imprison a single innocent one, no matter the procedural resources squandered. Accordingly this maxim, especially in light of its immense moral import, is suspect, and should be extended to include all palpable moral wrongs rather than only those recognized legally, albeit at times ineffectively. Of course, this position is not nearly as radical as it at first appears, for it is the subtle brilliance of the common law system which has permitted the unceasing legerdemain of judges throughout the centuries inventing new causes of action, despite their self-effacing claims of only modifying or reinterpreting existing ones. No better instance of this deftness of distinction can be found than in the seminal judgment of Lord Holt CJ in his dissent (later upheld in the House of Lords) in *Ashby v White* (1703), where Mr Ashby was denied the right to vote owing to the misfeasance of a public officer. Considerable debate surrounded whether the House of Commons maintained the right to resolve such disputes or whether authority should be ceded to the courts.

As Lord Holt eloquently summed up:

> If the plaintiff has a right, he must of necessity have a means to vindicate and maintain it...indeed it is a vain thing to imagine a right without a remedy; for want of right and want of remedy are reciprocal...And I am of opinion, that this action on the case is a proper action. My brother Powell J indeed thinks, that an action upon the case is not maintainable, because here is no hurt or damage to the plaintiff; but surely every injury imports a damage, though it does not cost the party one farthing, and it is impossible to prove the contrary; for a damage is not merely pecuniary, but an injury imports a damage, when a man is thereby hindered of his right.[1]

Knowing full well the procedural limitations of any immediate implementation of a scheme which would prohibit uncontroversially immoral, albeit not illegal, activity, such would not be the proposal herein advocated. Rather, we seek a progressive and staged approach toward this end, and one not so ambitious as to include within its orbit all *potentially* morally-questionable activity, but rather those infractions occasioning the most conspicuous disregard for moral obligation. Fortunately, few lacunae such as these still exist[2] per the bourgeoned expansion of the law's reach and the increasing number of offences it seeks to regulate; like all subjects apt to evolution, new and inventive means to evade legal enforcement will prevail temporarily. A fine

---

1 (1703) 92 ER 126, 137-139
2 One such example might include the greater availability to recover damages for mental distress and psychological injury following breach of contract or an extended duty of care, as the law in this regard is currently severely limited.

balance must therefore be struck between upholding the moral enforceability of *ubi jus ibi remedium* and not unwittingly creating *ex post facto* law. The cutting edge of science makes for a barbed thorn in the side of law's futile quest for certainty and exhaustiveness; issues involving therapeutic cloning and biometric information ownership will prove as fierce a battleground in the future as now-stale debates once did, themselves ranging widely from euthanasia and capital punishment to constitutional reform and international legal obligations. However, owing to the well-defined areas which attract the attention of equity, such as proprietary interest and trust relationships (and without the slightest hint of any madcap proposal to expand them!), the uncertainties associated with developing areas of law are absent in comparison, and therefore the force of the aforesaid arguments in favor of substantive justice serving to guide our maxim rather than reliance upon the pre-existing legal edifice for future guidance amid new and murky dilemmas is renewed.

He That Is Without Sin

The chronological scope of equity looks beyond the present, insistent that the past behavior of the parties to a dispute ought to be relevant to on-going proceedings. A moral dimension is added to this time frame; specifically, that any claimant seeking relief from the court must do so with clean hands. This is not to say that trivial wrongdoing shall incur the full wrath of equity insofar as it provides no relief, as in *Fiona Trust v Privalov* (2008), a case concerning fraudulent non-disclosure of documents and secret investigations into the directorship of two Russian shipping companies. However, non-negligible misconduct relevant to the otherwise successful invocation of equitable relief shall bar it, as in *Cross v Cross* (1983), where the claimant was denied specific performance of a contract brought about by his own fraudulent misrepresentation. Another instance of taking past blameworthy conduct into account in denying relief occurred in *D & C Builders Ltd v Rees* (1965), where Lord Denning refused to invoke equitable estoppel so as to prevent the claimant build-ers from receiving the full sum due for their work, despite their having previously settled for a lesser amount. It was determined that the defendant took advantage of the claimant's financial dif-ficulty so as to strong-arm them into such a lopsided and unfa-vorable arrangement.

Another instance of this maxim in operation came about in the colorful 19th-century case of *Lee v Haley* (1869), illustrative of the extent to which equity will be invoked to deter wrongdoing, however subtle its form. The plaintiffs were based in Pall Mall, running the successful "Guinea Coal Company." A disgruntled former employee thereafter set up a rival business named the "Pall Mall Guinea Coal Company at No. 46, Pall Mall" (the ad-dress of his former employer was No. 22). The plaintiffs, duly concerned that the similarity in names would siphon off lucra-tive customer contracts, sought an injunction to restrain the de-fendants from using the aforesaid name or any variant thereon. In the Court of Appeal in Chancery the defendant's appeal was dismissed, citing that *though the plaintiff had no legal right* to use his name, the lower court had properly ruled in his favor, owing to the malevolent motives of his former employee. Not only was motive rather than legal right taken into account in deciding the case, but the plaintiff did not need to show actual harm (*e.g.*, actual customers who had been deceived by the rival business and whose business was therefore lost by the plaintiffs). Inter-estingly, equity is flexible enough to look past not only the ab-sence of loss in still providing a remedy so long as there has been unconscionable dealing (as in the above case), but also where the claimant is guilty of wrongdoing generally, albeit not in re-gard to his specific cause of action. In *Tinsley v Milligan* (1994), the House of Lords ruled that a proprietary interest obtained during an illegal transaction (in this case, benefit fraud) could be none-theless valid so long as the specific illegality in question was not relied upon in the proceedings. Here, despite the collusion of two same-sex partners to maximize their welfare payments by keeping title to their house in only one of their names (despite both having contributed to the purchase price), because this crime was not necessary to invoke proprietary estoppel (once the legal titleholder unjustly sought complete possession of the house), a resulting trust was validly formed for the benefit of the partner without legal title.

On the face of it, this is a laudable maxim in that it consolidates the nexus between moral desert and the availability of legal remedy. Of course, there are limits to the insights any man may gain into his brother's motive, let alone the aloof monolith of the law. Accordingly, it is sensible to confine such investigations into those matters which are both germane and conducive to evidential corroboration; mere rumor as to the virtue or ignominy of an individual is a menace to any court attempting practical justice. As was so pithily captured by Associate Justice Louis Brandeis, "Equity does not demand that its suitors shall have led blameless lives."[1] It may be argued that so long as there is evidential verification as to the *general* disrepute of a man's character, then its lack of germaneness to the *given* proceeding should be irrelevant. This stimulates an uneasy debate regarding the proper and overarching role of our legal system. While its utmost charge is the realization of justice, it remains philosophically untenable (let alone practicably *impossible*, and not merely problematic) to permit the judgment of a man's generic character and rule accordingly pursuant to the instigation of a very specific dispute. The grounds for this position are multifarious; that no single party is privy to the conduct—let alone its best and fairest interpretation—as evinced by any person toward all others with whom he engages, throughout both time and place; that the nature of much of our behavior and its contemporaneous mental state are not subject to external verification, and/or via evidence not saturated by what would normally constitute supremely prejudicial material; and not least because a man's character may change suddenly, either toward good or evil, and

---

1 *Loughran v. Loughran*, 292 U.S. 216, 229

therefore is never, prior to his final breath, apt for accurate, all-encompassing judgment. A judge, however herculean his aspirant labors for incising impartiality, is still a man and never to be a god. Of course, a point such as this is primarily academic, but depleting its philosophical potency, however latent, is nevertheless useful in reaffirming the unconditional rectitude of this maxim. Duly, the jurisprudential soundness of equating legal remedy with relevant moral history remains one of the great and admirable hallmarks of equity law.

Whereas the courts invoking this maxim look to the past conduct of the claimant, his future conduct remains relevant in their determination of an equitable outcome. To that end, equity supplies additional useful guidelines, the first of which estimates the likeliest course of action taken by a claimant if supplied a remedy.

To Seek, to Strive, to Find

This maxim encapsulates the practical sense of justice replete in equitable maxims, insofar as one who "seeks equity must also do it." That is to say, simply initiating legal proceedings without a history of misconduct is insufficient; the court must be adequately convinced that if it provided a remedy favorable to the claimant, he must execute all associated obligations relevant to the effective and fair implementation of said remedy. For example, if the claimant sought specific performance of a contract, yet the court was unconvinced he either possessed the will or tangible resources to carry through with his promise, then it shall not award such a remedy. The same would apply in regard to an applicant seeking rescission; if he was unlikely to return any sums already paid to him as deposit following the withdrawal from the contract, the court will not rule in his favor.[1] The ratio-

---

1 A variation of this principle was embodied in *O'Sullivan v Management Agency and Music Ltd* (1985), involving the singer-songwriter Gilbert O'Sullivan who, in 1970 and without independent legal advice, entered into a heavily lopsided contract in favor of his record producer. Following a series of massively successful records, O'Sullivan claimed

nale is unshakable; the rulings of any court of equity take into account the conduct of the claimant as much as the defendant when determining the most just outcome between them. The efficacy of equitable maxims as vehicles for ensuring practical justice operates to the extent of the good character of the parties involved; therefore, the courts are wary as to the exploitation of their willingness for leniency by underhanded practitioners.

The boundaries of this maxim are not confined solely to the impact upon the defendant following a claimant's successful application for relief; rather, they extend to include the overarching demands that equity, as a set of general principles, must allow. This was amply demonstrated in *Jennings v Rice* (2002), where the Court of Appeal ruled that following the establishment of proprietary estoppel, the scope of its application was dictated by a wide judicial discretion designed to consider both the value of detriment suffered by the claimant as well as his expectations. However, whereupon the latter exceeded what was reasonably assumable or vastly disproportionate to the market value of his detriment, then equity would intervene to ensure a balance between these competing criteria. In this case, the appellant, who had labored for nearly thirty years for the now-deceased Mrs Royle (and who was suing the administrator of her estate) in various capacities as gardener, errand-boy and eventual live-in caretaker, sought entitlement to her valuable property and the furniture contained therein. This followed her oral promise to him that "he would be alright" and that "this will all [her estate] be yours one day." The entirety of the estate was valued at

---

a just proportion of the income he had generated; the management company admitted undue influence but refused to pay the appropriate percentage of profits back to the plaintiff. Though entitled in theory to *restitutio in integrum*, this option was unavailable as the contract had already been performed. Nonetheless, equity permits the court to implement a crude approximation of this remedy, insofar as the parties' contract could be set aside despite the impossibility of returning them to their exact pre-contractual positions. Rather, a compromise was forged, permitting O'Sullivan some £7 million in damages, whilst also allowing the company to retain both reasonable compensation and profit for having made the singer a star.

well over £1 million. The High Court had ruled that such a figure was greatly in excess of the value of Mr Jennings's services,
and thereupon awarded him the sum of £200,000. The Court of
Appeal concurred, Walker LJ delivering the following pellucid
opinion:

> 'It is no coincidence that these statements of princi-
> ple refer to satisfying the equity (rather than satisfying,
> or vindicating, the claimant's expectations). The equity
> arises not from the claimant's expectations alone, but
> from the combination of expectations, detrimental reli-
> ance, and the unconscionableness of allowing the bene-
> factor (or the deceased benefactor's estate) to go back
> on the assurances...
>
> To recapitulate: there is a category of case in which
> the benefactor and the claimant have reached a mutual
> understanding which is in reasonably clear terms but
> does not amount to a contract. In such a case the court's
> natural response is to fulfil the claimant's expectations.
> But if the claimant's expectations are uncertain, or
> extravagant, or out of all proportion to the detriment
> which the claimant has suffered, the court can and
> should recognise that the claimant's equity should be
> satisfied in another (and generally more limited) way.
>
> But that does not mean that the court should in
> such a case abandon expectations completely, and look
> to the detriment suffered by the claimant as defining
> the appropriate measure of relief. Indeed in many cases
> the detriment may be even more difficult to quantify,
> in financial terms, than the claimant's expectations...
> Moreover the claimant may not be motivated solely
> by reliance on the benefactor's assurances, and may re-
> ceive some countervailing benefits (such as free bed and
> board). In such circumstances the court has to exercise

a wide judgmental discretion."[1]

The above goes so far as to forcefully indicate that equity is concerned more with the independent and just valuation of labor and reliance than it is with the agreed appraisals as made between the parties (however informally). Normally, the bounds of equitable intervention stop short of interfering with the sanctity of freedom to contract, but of course, this unrestrained legal right has been greatly curtailed by such legislation as the Unfair Contract Terms Act 1977, the Contracts (Rights of Third Parties) Act 1999 and the Unfair Terms in Consumer Contracts Regulations 1999, the latter giving domestic force to the EU Unfair Consumer Contract Terms Directive 93/13/EEC. Undoubtedly, these developments and the specific steps taken to ameliorate the previous absence of legal remedy were strongly colored by equitable doctrine.

Words as Bonds

More dryly expressed as equity's "imputation of an intention to fulfill an obligation", this guideline captures the oddly consequentialist attitude taken by equity under certain circumstances. Often with its emphasis upon principle at the expense of logistical certainty, equity is less concerned with bureaucratic efficiency than it is a just outcome. This maxim does not represent an exception to that rule insofar as it seeks the establishment of justice between the parties, though it is willing to arrive at such an end, in a rare departure, by occasionally disregarding their intentions.

Sowden v Sowden (1875) involved a debtor who failed to discharge his debt whilst alive, and who, upon death, had an outstanding creditor. In his will, he bequeathed a legacy to his creditor, deemed by the court as a gift, which, although not perfect performance of his legal obligation, was deemed sufficiently near it in nature and purpose as to adequately discharge the debt. Ac-

---

1 [2002] EWCA 159 [49-51]

cordingly, the creditor was unable to both keep the legacy and sue for the debt unpaid during the debtor's lifetime.

There are certain instances in which the law will demand complete performance (*e.g.*, the exercise of an option), though these are relatively rare. As succinctly stated by Sir Lloyd Kenyon MR: "The principle is, that 'where a man covenants to do an act, and he does an act which may be converted to a completion of this covenant, it shall be supposed that he meant to complete it.'"[1] To this extent, equity is once more concerned with substance over form, even in those cases where determination of the former may be satisfied without the prior intent toward achieving said effect by the parties. Such contrivance is aimed at preventing overcompensation of the covenantee rather than safeguarding the rights of those already burdened by their legal obligations.

This precept is philosophically sound as regards delimiting the margin of gain attainable by the promisee, though potentially less so as regards respecting the wishes (especially postmortem) of the promisor. Usually, in the absence of explicit testamentary disposition, an intention to fulfill one's obligations is necessary such that practical justice may be done; however, in circumstances whereupon the deceased promisor has explicitly left his estate to a non-creditor, despite the existence of outstanding debts to be paid, such creditors as may decide to enforce payment must remain unable to "hopscotch" over the necessary legal proceedings to ensure due payment of their loans, especially when at the expense of the rightful (that is, named) beneficiaries. That is, to use this maxim of equity as a shortcut disapplying the explicit will of the promisor would be an abandonment of due legal process and unjustly enhance the position of these creditor-promisees, especially where the rights of a creditor have been at best *prima facie* unascertained (at least initially) and at worst diminished by misconduct or the presence of others outranking in priority. Equally, such misuse

1 (1785) 1 Cox's Chancery Cases 165

would disregard the premium placed by equity on the intent of the parties, especially those whose rights are less secure following death.

Extinction of Forfeiture

Forfeiture entails the uncompensated loss of the exercise of one's legal rights subsequent to a failure to perform a previously agreed obligation, such as the surrendering of one's interest in real estate or bar to claiming the benefits of a breached contract. This is so even if the triggering violation is negligible and the lost right in question significant—say, constructing an entire and otherwise-perfect swimming pool (albeit a few inches shallower than originally specified), and this minor breach releasing the user from having to pay for *any* portion of its construction.[1] The relevance of forfeiture, however, is best seen in cases involving mortgages, in which the most draconian form of extinguishment of accrued proprietary interest (usually instant and irreversible) is known as foreclosure. The payments made by a mortgagor throughout the course of his mortgage account for the accrual of his equity against the debt first secured by the bank which loaned the capital necessary to purchase the property. Originally, this was not the case. Instead, the mortgagor had very little security over his land, and, upon a single failing to repay his periodic loan (with interest), the mortgagee could not only entirely revoke his proprietary interest over his home but also keep the sums paid toward discharge of the mortgage debt—even if only one payment short of completion. Inevitably, debtors would default, pleading for leniency before the chancery court, which frequently permitted ownership over the land to return to the borrower so long as he honored his debts—that is, the court would *not* disregard the sums already paid to the mortgagee as partial entitlement to the land. So long as there was no undue delay in the payment of these debts, the courts of equity would often find sympathy for the underdog borrower.

1 *Ruxley Electronics and Construction Ltd v Forsyth* [1995] UKHL 8

In time, this equitable exception became the rule, such that no court of conscience would permit the inequitable extinction of a mortgagor's proprietary interest. In an effort to rebalance the rights between lenders and borrowers, bills of foreclosure were introduced which permitted a mortgagee to bar the mortgagor of all title to, and equity of redemption in, his premises if the debt was not fully discharged by the legal due date. Understandably, courts of equity are extremely reluctant to grant this option, especially when a significant portion, if not the entire, debt may be satisfied either through granting the mortgagor additional time to repay on his loan or, in more desperate instances, the approval of a forced sale. Even in the latter case, however, the mortgagor is entitled to be repaid a sum equivalent to his equity in the property following the repayment of any hitherto debt owned by the lending bank. Without question, the transformation of equitable exceptionalism into the norm as regards the mortgagor's rights under a mortgage are to be hailed as a great step taken toward the coincidence of land law and commonsensical morality. That a man's labors, the fruits of which are no more readily apparent than in the land melded with his very sweat, must not be deprived their just due by technicality or the superior legal armory of a lending bank, is the truest principle enshrined in the evaporation of this once most harsh common law state of affairs.

Defense of the mortgagor's rights cannot be unlimited, however, especially where he has managed his finances recklessly. To extend the protection afforded by our maxim to the profligate and shortsighted would have calamitous consequences for homeownership at large, as banks would be devoid the requisite legal assurances of enforcing their claims whenever a mortgagor defaulted on his loans. Accordingly, whilst a balance must be struck, as in all matters of principle, the pendulum should swing decidedly in the favor of the borrower, whose relatively limited resources shall always predispose banks toward predatory lending practices which offer him all too often inadequate protection against the enforcement of the latter's strict legal rights, especially when such constitutes a direct threat to his domiciliary security.

That equity abhors a forfeiture extends beyond the domain of land alone. With its distaste for any loophole to trump the substantive rights of a party, the erasure of forfeiture encompasses not only resistance to the termination of a mortgage but also provisions fairly bargained for in a contract. Equity is reluctant to set aside an entire contract for a minor breach, unless such was the explicit intention of both parties, whereupon this maxim is outranked by "equity following the law." Regardless, non-proprietary forfeiture seldom incurs the same penalty as exacted in foreclosure proceedings, especially when economic interest in the former may be restored upon payment with interest, whereas such is impossible under the latter scenario, the harshness of which has seen its near-extinction in favor of extending a mortgagor's redemption date or forced sale of the property. The aim of either alternative remains the avoidance of the borrower's equity being unfairly extinguished, and even more dramatically, the occupant being turned out into the street.

This maxim accordingly occasions brief discussion on the centrality of human rights to the operation of equitable precepts generally, but especially those concerning property ownership. This is highlighted by Article 8 of the European Convention on Human Rights, the right to respect for private and family life (including one's home and correspondence) and Article 1 of Protocol 1, the right to the peaceful enjoyment of one's possessions. A series of cases have sought to clarify the meaning and extent of the latter, not least owing to the grounds for permissible derogation contained in the text itself. These generally justify exceptions to the blanket prohibition on deprivation of property only in times of genuine public interest, and never to the extent that the victim is uncompensated for his economic loss. Section 2 of the Article makes clear that in no way does the aforesaid diminish the power of the State to either enforce taxation or to control the use of property for the greater good, namely planning purposes. The European Court of Human Rights (ECHR) has construed the meaning of "possessions" widely, including both tangible and intangible types of property, the latter group including contractual arrangements, pensions and capital stock. Altogether, modern human rights jurisprudence has converged to attain many of the same goals as equity, protection of proprietary interest being amongst them. Of course, while the protection (and just distribution) of property has always remained at the heart of English equity law, it appears to remain a secondary right as viewed by ECHR jurisprudence when compared to those pertaining directly to freedoms of the person.

Contra Fraud

That equity abhors the perversion of any statute toward unconscionable or iniquitous ends is among the more obvious maxims. As was so masterly summed up by Denning LJ in *Lazarus Estates v Beasley*: "Fraud unravels everything."[1] In that case, what would have otherwise proved a procedural bar to the defendant tenant claiming against the fraudulent declaration by his landlord as to repairs performed on his property (specifically, lapse of deadline to challenge the declaration) was deemed a nullity and held to be void, the appeal being heard and a new trial thereafter ordered. Every effort is made to cure the poisoning influence of fraud, and this even includes preventing a party from being able to rely on his strict legal rights when to do so would offend the conscience of equity. This safeguard comes into operation whenever an attempt is made to exploit the absence of statutory formalities so as to engineer an unjust outcome as regards contracts of land, the creation of express trusts and legal leases and registering land charges.

Moreover, this maxim is used to justify the existence of "secret trusts," testamentary arrangements in which the settlor posthumously communicates his desire to attach certain condi-

1 [1956] 1 QB 702 at 712

tions to a legacy, namely that the legatee (usually his solicitor) holds property confidentially on trust for a third party. Essentially, their function is to shield the identity of the beneficiary from becoming known, a form of non-disclosure which assumes enhanced importance following probate whereupon a will becomes a part of the public record. There are two types of secret trusts: "fully secret" and "half-secret." Whereas the former completely hides any indication of a trust existing in the will, the latter discloses the existence of the trust, but not its terms or beneficiaries. Both types of secret trust are enforced so as to prevent fraud; the risk of misconduct is especially obvious as concerns fully secret trusts, whereby the trustee may attempt to keep the trust property for himself, in clear violation of his fiduciary duties to the beneficiary. Although the Wills Act 1837 requires certain formalities to be present in order to validate any trust (*viz.* written documentation, signature and witness attestation), the legislation does not apply to secret trusts; thus, a secret trustee cannot rely on the absence of formality to fraudulently acquire trust property. This logic is increasingly strained however concerning half-secret trusts, because barring the court's refusal to review the actual terms of the trust, the trustee could only hold the property on resulting trust for the beneficiary, thereby being unable to commit fraud inasmuch as the beneficiary is deprived of his bequest. Rather, the view forwarded in *Blackwell v Blackwell* (1929) explains the creation of the trust as a creature operating outside of the will itself, instead generated through the relationship shared between settlor and trustee, the latter undertaking a personal obligation to the former which is triggered upon his death. This convoluted logic attempts to reconcile the continuation of secret trusts as legal devices with a creative means of preventing fraud, even in the absence of statutory formalities.

Of course, the ambit of equity's suspicions of fraudulent dealing, and its attempt to eliminate its effects, extend beyond the realm of secret trusts. One particularly informative case is *Bannister v Bannister* (1948), the relevant facts being that an elderly widow inherited some property following her husband's death, and then conveyed it to her brother-in-law below market value on the oral understanding that she could reside there until her death. Following his attempt to evict her, and despite the bargain struck *not* otherwise being enforceable, equity intervened by imposing a constructive trust which permitted her to acquire a proprietary life interest. Here, the fraud was not in the undervaluation of the conveyance, but rather the denial of the trust itself. The Court of Appeal arguably went to greater lengths to prevent fraud in *Shah v Shah* (2001), whereby a witness to an improperly-construed deed sought to set it aside for personal gain. The court ruled that reliance on the defective document would constitute a fraud, and therefore instead upheld the deed, despite its imperfect formation. Considering the emphasis placed upon procedural formality in the construal of deeds, this decision forcefully demonstrates the court's abhorrence to permitting the use of any legal instrument as a vehicle for facilitating deceitful practice. As a maxim of equity, this lends special importance to our study as an instance where moral principle trumped the stringent requirements of legal technicality, where to abide by them would yield an unjust outcome.

Philosophically, the basis for this maxim is most sound, and *Shah v Shah* speaks to the priority given to upholding fair dealing even if at the cost of forgoing documentary certainty. Of course, the novel manifestation of this maxim applies insofar as it seeks to prevent the law itself from being used as a means of immorality, in addition to helping craft new laws whose very purpose is to dispel such dishonest practice. For this maxim ensures that the courts rather "self-destruct" any law tainted with complicity in inequitable dealing than uphold it so as to maintain administrative consistency. Such liberality in valuing principle over practicality is not shared in other areas of the law, where an emphasis is placed upon general certainty over justice in the specific case. Equally, fraud speaks to the very mischief that equity seeks to avoid: a concern with the inner intentions, rather than outer form, of actors' conduct. Whereas other subjects such as tort and contract, saturated with strict-liability regimes, resist so onerous an undertaking as divining the specific motivations of parties, equity's chief concern for fairness is fuelled by a stamina aimed at the discovery of such knowledge. The expenditure of effort required to gain insight and the subsequent bespoke remedies such information affords are consequently ill-suited for widespread application; such remedies are understandably offered only via the court's discretion and not as a matter of right.

However, the corrupting effects of fraud in the maintenance and efficacy of any legal regime are uniquely corrosive, and accordingly, if any perversion of the *telos* of law ought to trigger its bespoke rectification (as in the invocation of estoppel in *Shah* preventing reliance on the defective deed despite former representations made by the signatory party to the contrary), then surely fraud should qualify. The availability of remedy is made considerably easier under equity owing to the court being able to act *in personam*. The imposition of a constructive trust similarly proves a robust tool in ensuring that unauthorized profit on the part of the trustee[1] is held for the benefit of the beneficiary.[2] However, despite the onerous duties placed upon the former so as to prevent the occurrence of fraud (*e.g.,* the prohibition on the trustee from purchasing trust property in his own name, the so-called "rule against self-dealing"), it should be recalled that liability for breach of trust is strict in the sense that neither fault

---

1 Even strangers to the trust may be held liable as constructive trustees whereupon they undertake dishonest assistance of the trustees in breach of their fiduciary obligations. Per Lord Selborne LC in *Barnes v Addy* (1874): '...strangers are not made constructive trustees merely because they act as the agents of trustees...unless those agents receive and become chargeable with some part of the trust property, or unless they assist with knowledge in a dishonest and fraudulent design on the part of the trustees' (251-252).

2 As determined by the Court of Appeal in *Sinclair Investments v Versailles Trade Finance* (2011), there are limits to what a beneficiary may recover. Here, it was ruled that the beneficiary acquired no proprietary entitlement over a bribe received by the trustee, though was able to hold any assets acquired subsequent to the trustee's breach of fiduciary duties to equitable account.

nor intent are relevant. For, a trust imposes mandatory duties upon the trustee which must be executed, unlike dispositive powers, which are discretionary. Therefore, a willingness to prevent fraud at all costs may potentially create liability for trustees otherwise acting in *bona fide* good faith; however, the courts are reluctant to impose liability in the absence of sharp practice or exceptional circumstances.[1]

The law as it currently stands strikes what appears an appropriate balance between the court's powers to intervene pursuant to its aversion to fraud and maintaining the rights of trustees such that their discretion is not unduly fettered toward safeguarding the interests of their beneficiaries. Excessive oversight is only likely to produce a chilling effect as regards even minutely risky undertakings, and therefore trustees must be able to perform in confidence that barring egregious breaches of responsible conduct, liability for fraud is highly improbable. This is especially so when trustees are required to acquire a controlling shareholder interest in companies and thereafter usually expected to take an active role in the management of said company,[2] for here the importance of discretion is at a premium. The continuing role played by secret trusts is arguably anachronistic, especially in light of their commonest function historically (*i.e.*, the shielding from public record of dispositions made to the testator's mistress or illegitimate children), such that certainly as regards the half-secret trust, the logic of fraud avoidance is untenable, and in the case of fully-secret trusts, the risk of fraud occurring too great in the absence of documentary evidence. For both, that a fraudulent misallocation of beneficial interests between beneficiaries may occur is the best case scenario, that a trustee attempts to scamper off with the entirety of the property itself the worst. Accordingly, the future of this species of trust is to be doubted in light of equity's overarching concern for the prevention of fraud. Considering equity's preoc-

1 *Holder v Holder* [1968] Ch. 353
2 *Re Lucking's Will Trusts* [1967] 3 All ER 726

cupation with the moral conduct of the parties, the invocation of the "clean hands" maxim may further highlight the incongruity between its precepts and secret trusts insofar as the latter have previously facilitated immoral behavior by ensuring the anonymity of beneficiaries.

CHAPTER II: PROCEDURAL FORMALITY

AT FIRST BLUSH it might appear difficult to reconcile equitable maxims with the small-mindedness of mere procedure, especially when the latter conflicts with the substantive merits of a case. Admittedly, with equity's supreme concern for intent over form, there is an irreducible tension between these competing aims. However, of the following maxims to be analyzed, most attempt to ultimately appeal to the core issue of fair dealing *as regards the specific case*, unlike blanket rules imposed in other areas of law, such as unyielding protocols regarding evidence admission, time limitations or strict liability regimes, themselves the result of larger, socio-structural factors (*e.g.,* strict employer liability following from the availability of mass insurance policies) which may be wholly unconnected with the individual facts but rather aimed at resolving external demands placed upon the courts. These include not merely maximizing the bureaucratic efficiency with which cases may be accelerated through the docket, but restricting the "floodgates" of litigation as regard the creation of new duties of care. Such concerns were epitomized in the Compensation Act 2006 in its instruction to judges to take account of the chilling effect impositions of liability may create in discouraging otherwise worthwhile activities on the part of defendants, whether commercial or gratuitous. Equity generally resists taking such external considerations as fully into account in the development of even those maxims related to procedural efficiency.

Aiding the Vigilant

Vigilantibus non dormientibus æquitas subvenit—the vigilant are rewarded, not those who sleep on their rights. Not only is this clearly relevant toward ensuring procedural efficiency by imposing temporal limitations within which claims must be made (of additional value to the potential defendant such that he does not labor endlessly under the threatening specter of litigation), but invokes the practically just notion that the law requires some proactivity on the part of the victim; that not every injustice can be positively reacted to by the long arm of the law. Some degree of protest is required by the claimant, and that begins with his timely bringing of a suit. This further proves economically beneficial, for the greater the delay, the costlier the accrual of relevant evidence. Perhaps most imperiling is the decreasing accuracy of submitted evidence (particularly in the guise of witness testimony), thereby jeopardizing the likelihood of the court's basis for rendering a truly just outcome. Instead, the defendant is permitted to trigger an estoppel based upon laches.[1] As aforesaid, the concern of equity is responding to the merits of the individual case; therefore, unlike the universalized time deadline prescribed in a limitation act, laches is unique to the claimant party, and can apply even prior to the expiry of the limitation period, thereby raising the judicial inference of a weak claim on the claimant's part or a reluctance to sue.

Of course, that any court of equity would turn its back on supplying the claimant redress over mere delay appears to violate one of the most fundamental maxims: that equity will not

---

1 Laches as a bar to recovery was first recorded in *Chief Young Dede v. African Association Ltd.* (1910) 1 N.L.R 130 at 133.

suffer a wrong without providing a remedy. This tension appears to be irreconcilable, and considering that laches is invoked owing less to a concern for the logistical assurance of finality to proceedings (not least because equity is concerned with substance over form) and more due to a judicial suspicion of a claimant's motivation for delay, this maxim is ethically suspect. This is especially so considering that the merits of the claimant's case can readily be made out once litigation is initiated, and therefore judicial presumptions against him can only hamper the interests of justice.[1] It is inappropriate for equity, with its concern for idiographic justice, to apply logic similar to that of other areas of law (such as negligence in tort) to temporally limit the filing of lawsuits based exclusively on either reasons of public policy or, as is more likely in chancery, procedural efficiency. Resisting this trend is advisable especially in light of the inroads made by the Limitation Act 1980 in subsuming the relevance of this maxim. An exception to the otherwise unsuited combination of logistical concerns and the aims of equity is in regard to the availability of remedies, particularly Mareva (or freezing) injunctions, where excessive delay will engender the defeat of an application in the absence of compelling evidence, not least because of the oppressive effects incurred in the control of use of the defendant's assets for a sustained period.[2]

---

1 However, a promising reversal to this presumption was introduced in *Hughes v La Baia Ltd* (2007), where the Privy Council indicated that the onus is upon the defendant to prove that the claimant should not be entitled to relief despite delay.

2 In *Cherney v Neuman* (2009), the High Court rightly concluded that an eight-month delay in the application for a worldwide freezing injunction should be denied, belying the claimant's fear of the urgent risk of the disposal of assets. Similarly, any form of non-disclosure on the part of the claimant in not supplying the court with the necessary information required in its sober assessment as to whether the granting of an injunction on his behalf is not unduly onerous upon the defendant will result in the dismissal of such application. Per Lord Denning in *Third Chandris Shipping Corporation v Unimarine SA* (1979), the plaintiff is required to disclose all relevant and material facts to the court so as to permit its proper exercise over invoking the freezing injunctions (668-669).

In loco procurator

Again, the fusion of concern for procedural formality and at least partial regard to the moral obligation of continuing to enforce the intentions of the testator is found in our next maxim—that a trust shall not fail for want of a trustee. The absence of a trustee can occur for all sorts of reasons, from voluntary action to removal under jurisdiction by the court.[1] Initially, whereupon no trustee is located or the court does not make an appointment, he with legal title to the trust property occupies the role. It should be recalled that any individual with recognized legal capacity may serve as a trustee, including a trust corporation. While minors are frequently identified as the exceptions to this rule, they can nonetheless maintain legal title as either resulting or constructive trustees, as established in *Re Vinogradoff* (1935).[2]

While the maxim itself is generally uncontroversial, the extent to which trusts may fail for want of other, equally technical, reasons is a source of criticism, specifically in the context of the certainty of the intentions of the settlor. No more is this evident than as concerns charitable trusts, where the requisite exclusivity of the charitable intentions of the testator has unnecessarily led to the voiding of a great number of otherwise worthwhile bequests for the public benefit. This requirement proves an obstacle not only owing to the impossibility of perfectly capturing a man's intentions even in the most scrupulously prepared testamentary disposition, but further in the inability of the courts to seek his clarification, for all such disputes are postmortem. Even the cy-près doctrine, aimed at ensuring the effectuation of the spirit of the trust, is unhelpful insofar as a preliminary charitable intention is required if there is no subsequent failing of the operation of the trust.

1 Jurisdiction is both inherent and statutory, the latter via s.41 of the Trustee Act 1925. Further, the Charity Commission has similar jurisdiction as the High Court under the Charities Act 1993.
2 The ambit of this ruling is limited by s.20 of the Law of Property Act 1925, whereby minors cannot serve as trustees over land.

Further, considering the emphasis placed upon the settlor's intentions, the current law is unsatisfactory as the current safeguards do not prevent the court appointment of inappropriate trustees to manage trust property. As replaced trustees need not be consulted regarding court appointments (even where their replacement is not due to wrongful conduct), there is the substantial risk that a new appointment will be inappropriate, owing to unfamiliarity with the nature of the trust or ensuring due care for the beneficiaries, especially in the absence of a long-forged relationship. This occurred in *Re Tempest* (1866), where the Court of Appeal remarkably stated that reluctance on the part of existing co-trustees to collaborate with a new court appointment would not necessarily alter its selection, and might in fact serve as a positive ground for their own removal. It is herein argued that reform is necessary ensuring a widening of the cy-près doctrine, whereupon in cases of initial failure a general charitable intention is not required, as such is captured in the benefit to be conferred by the bequest itself (if that was of a non-charitable aim, then of course the doctrine should not apply). Moreover, judicial appointment of trustees should not only take account of the explicit intentions of the testator, but the more practical developments thereafter, such as beneficiary-trustee relations and the recent history of trust direction (including investment, provision of maintenance and advancement, etc.), so as to minimize disruption following the selection of a new appointment (whose approach toward managing the trust should align itself with that undertaken hitherto), demonstrating greater deference to those parties intimately connected to the daily operation of the trust—namely, the currently acting co-trustees and beneficiaries, the latter especially in instances of their being *sui juris* and evidently responsible in their hitherto dealings with trust property.

Limiting Litigation

Whilst at first appearance this maxim may appear to be

uniquely devoid of moral substance, such is untrue, not principally because of the end achieved (for that is rather obviously beneficial in terms of procedural efficiency), but rather the underpinning rationale unique to its equitable application. The principle is best manifested when multiple parties, all related to a common source of grievance, appear before the court, the latter being able to issue a judgment relevant to each in one sitting, thereby forestalling the possibility of subsequent multiple lawsuits initiated by those not litigants in the present case. The maxim is most regularly invoked in the civil procedure known as interpleader and the arcane practice known as Bill of Peace, of which shall be focused upon owing to their equitable roots. Moreover, the class action is often justified in terms of reducing superfluous claims from clogging the docket.

Interpleader actions are especially useful in insurance disputes where the plaintiff (so named because the defendants are in fact referred to as claimants) or "stakeholder," holding property belonging to another, unascertained party, is permitted to legally compel two or more additional parties to enter the dispute so that the court may identify its rightful owner. During this period of unascertained ownership, the court usually holds on trust the property. Although originally a common law remedy, it evolved into an equitable one, usually requiring

a) that all parties have a viable stake in the property in dispute, that dispute being the common link between the defendants being compelled to litigate, and

b) the stakeholder must be a neutral party, free of any liability to the parties. Sensibly, the jurisdiction of the court was widened under the Common Law Procedures Act 1860, allowing the interpleading of claims even where potential title to the property emerged from conflicting sources. By doing so, the power to reduce multiple lawsuits was made even more robust.

However, a principled basis can be found for this judicial creation. Where an insurer, for instance, was exposed to paying out upon a claim, but the circumstances surrounding it were dubious (*e.g.*, foul play, self-inflicted injury, etc.), and yet not in positive possession of any proof against it, the court via an interpleader action may hear the evidence compelled by potential beneficiaries. To this extent, the blameless stakeholder need not undergo the onerous burden of remaining a litigant or incurring further financial expenditure (his attorney's fees payable by the defendants). Not only does this vehicle permit the most efficient allocation of court time and resources toward considering the merits of, and applying the judgment to, the case as most clearly understood via the germane evidence supplied by *all relevant parties*, but reduces needless aggravation on the part of the impartial stakeholder who is necessarily without liability (where he is otherwise, the court may rightly find outstanding obligations on his part to the defendants). Of course, this process also expedites the processing of claims, thereby reducing the strain placed upon both judicial attention toward more pressing and complex suits and the public purse in financing the operation of the justice system.

The ancient Bill of Peace is an instrument similar in function. Originally developed by the Court of Chancery over four centuries ago, it joined a multitude of parties to a dispute per common features shared between them, the decision rendered duly binding them all, even if any party opted out of actively participating in the proceedings. Until the merger of equity and common law in the 1870s, only equitable remedies such as the injunction were available. Following the Judicature Acts, common law damages also became available to claimants.

Lastly, turning to the class suit, the advantage to this avenue is, most obviously, the integration of multiple (in some cases, thousands) of claims against the same defendant(s). Historically, English courts assumed the right of plaintiffs to represent non-litigating parties, so long as the plaintiff avowed such others held similar interests in the case; such class suits eventually fell under the purview of the chancery courts. Today, evidence of more personal involvement is required in order to join as a claimant. Additional advantages include the greater incentive for individual claimants to participate by reducing the opportunity cost of litigation; if successful in damages, then this far more massive sum (relative to an individual claimant securing a favorable verdict) may alter those practices by the defendant which first triggered the litigation. Toward these ends, equity provides a toolbox of solutions which, guided by the interests of achieving individual justice and, in some cases, altering systemically abusive behavior on the part of defendants, furnishes potent remedies aligned with ensuring procedural efficiency. This fusion of benefits differs from the often policy-oriented rules in place in other areas of law concerned exclusively with promoting the expeditious handling of heavy caseloads.

Ceteris paribus, legal interest will prevail

There is significant overlap between this maxim and another to be discussed, that of "equity following the law." Equitable relief emerged historically so as to make available remedies considered necessary in order to ameliorate the often-harsh inflexibility of the common law. However, there were limits to the extent even the chancery courts would travel in disregarding the more rigid structure of their common law counterpart. This was partly to ensure that equity as an alternate legal forum did not wholly displace the common law, and because the latter, owing to its universalized approach to dispute resolution, was far better able to handle the vast majority of cases, since the bespoke approach taken by equity, being considerably more laborious, could only be applied in the minority of cases which uniquely offended intuitive sensibilities of justice and the generally sufficient framework of the common law. Moreover, proprietary legal rights, whilst not as perceptive of conscionable entitlement as equity, are nevertheless superior as regards their binding quality, which is against the world at large, rather than equity whose rights bite only against the far narrower category of a bona fide purchaser for value without notice (of the other party's right to title), or so-called "Equity's Darling."

Accordingly, equity shall do nothing in vain, and most certainly so where there is no moral, let alone legally recognized,
wrong to rectify. The domain of equity is the softening of a legal
ruling; where no legal cause of action existed, equity could not be
of assistance; it served merely to supplant the unyielding rigor of
those remedies first applied by the common law. While this was
logistically understandable, there is no principled basis for this
maxim, not least because of the conscience-guided jurisdiction
of equity. Equity, as a domain of law, is best manifested not as a
supplement to the common law but rather as a refining modifier
capable of not only perfecting specific injustices but shaping the
very future direction of the course taken by the latter. To this
end, equity ought to serve as an experimental spearhead upon
which subsequent developments in the law should first be tested via individual cases brought before its jurisdiction owing to
the failing of the common law, and, if reforms proposed are both
principled and systemically viable, they should be introduced so
as to alter the actual substance of the common law. This fusion
is perfectly implementable, as both systems have been procedur-
ally, if not substantively, fused following the Supreme Court of
Judicature Acts of 1873 and 1875.[1]

Ceteris paribus, earlier interest will prevail

Amongst the simplest maxims to grasp, where there are
two conflicting equitable interests, otherwise equal in moral

---

1 The extent of substantive fusion between the common law and equity is disputed. In *United Scientific Holdings Ltd v Burnley Borough Council*
[1978] AC 904, Lord Denning suggested that, '...by the Judicature Act
1873 the two systems of substantive and adjectival law formerly administered by Courts of Law and Courts of Chancery were fused' (924-
925). However, it is herein held that a more accurate depiction is the
procedural fusion expressed by Somers J in *Elders Pastoral Ltd v Bank of
New Zealand* [1989] 2 NZLR 180, 'the fact that both are administered
by one Court has inevitably meant that each has borrowed from the
other in furthering the harmonious development of the law' (193). In
his view, the separation of legal and equitable rights, interests and remedies prevents substantive fusion from being possible. This view proves
ultimately more compelling.

standing, the earliest in time will prevail. Any pollution of the morally-binding essence of an equitable interest will ensure that its competitor is prioritized (*e.g.,* where he who invokes the sullied interest comes to court with unclean hands, does not intend to honor his obligations, etc.). That the earliest prevails is not justifiable only as an arbitrary means of resolving an otherwise deadlocked dispute; the popular sentiment "possession is nine-tenths of the law" may be applied so as to understand law generally, and particularly English land and equity law, as uniquely concerned with the factual state of affairs present between the parties outside of court. Accordingly, he who has the earlier claim has enjoyed a longer period in which it has reified, arguably making its possession more real and inseparable from his legal and psychological identity than that of his challenger. This labor-theory of entitlement features prominently in land law, equity's cousin, enunciated lucidly in Locke's *Two Treatises of Civil Government,* where he argued that all land was to be viewed as the magnanimous gift of God, appropriated by individual men only through the fusion of their individual efforts with the soil itself. Through this amalgam of labor and land emerged proprietary ownership.

CHAPTER III: GUIDING PRINCIPLES

THE FIRST TWO CHAPTERS of this book have examined the interrelationship between the evolution and instruments of equity as regard first its substantive content, followed by the procedural guidelines by which such substance is often implemented. In this last section dedicated principally to focused critiques of specific aspects of equity law as it currently stands, those final maxims which fall into neither of the aforesaid categories shall be examined. This last group refers neither to the heart of equity's moral conscience nor the rules of mere procedure, but rather those guidelines which facilitate principled outcomes by virtue of extralegal practical considerations. To this extent, these last six maxims straddle both camps, their means reflected in procedure, their ends in fair dealing. We begin with one of the most powerful tools in the arsenal of equity—its capacity to tailor court remedies to resolve disputes between the specific litigants in question.

In Personam

That equity is chiefly concerned with rectifying the morally blameworthy conduct of the defendant himself is exemplified in this maxim. Chancery courts have long been preoccupied with ensuring enforcement of their edicts against a specific individual, thereby requiring flexibility in the range of remedies available in the resolution of oftentimes complex disputes. What this array of remedies retains in common is an abhorrence of unconscionable conduct, and the aim of both punishing and correcting it. Injunctions, court-ordered specific performance, and search orders are amongst the tools at hand for responding to the defendant's wrongful conduct.

So august is the will of equity to see justice done that jurisdictional constraints can be set aside in certain circumstances. For instance, *Penn v Lord Baltimore* (1750) affirmed the court's capacity to resolve a land dispute notwithstanding the property in question being outside England (in this case, a provincial boundary between the then-colonies of Pennsylvania and Maryland). The plaintiff's request for specific performance of delimiting boundaries was granted, with the agreement struck between the parties deemed reviewable as both were in the jurisdiction of the court, even if the subject matter of the dispute was not (*i.e.*, the land itself). The case also prominently demonstrates the lengths to which equity will intervene in the resolution of even technical disputes; this case is noted for its complexity not merely owing to jurisdictional concerns, but the panoply of unorthodox evidence which required assessment by the court. Such included balancing cartographic, political and proprietary issues ranging from the effects of a royal grant abroad to the legal entitlements of plantation settlers to inaccuracies regarding latitudinal measurements between the boundaries. Nevertheless, equity was determined to fashion a remedy. The same holds true for trusts, where a trustee may be held personally liable for a breach of fiduciary duty. To this end, the court may grant a freezing injunction over his assets, even if located abroad. The penalties for non-compliance are similarly vigorous, including being held in contempt of court and imprisonment.

The bespoke nature of equitable remedies deserves commendation, an exemplar of an otherwise aloof legal edifice able to furnish unique solutions to alleviate the anguishes of the claimant. Amongst the most recurring tensions found in our contemporary legal corpus is the one between ensuring certainty through the universality of edicts and the nomothetic means for their resolution, and justice in the individual case, whereby its unique facts often prevent the application of blanket rules which disregard the criticality of nuances of fact and circumstance. It must not be forgotten that law and ethics are two separate domains, and whatever the urges to elevate the former toward the same heights as the latter, a variety of sociostructural constraints make such an ambition utterly utopian. Amongst the most pressing is the overwhelming bureaucratization of law as a social institution, a process meted out almost in assembly-line fashion across hundreds of thousands of cases annually, ranging from such diverse matters as petty crimes to multi-billion pound trust disputes, constitutional infringements to the interpretation of statutory instruments. Ethics is necessarily a personal affair, one which appeals to and informs the sensibilities of individual conscience; law is a far blunter tool, able to deliver only a crude approximation of the directives of even the most comprehensive moral framework, whose efficacy is ultimately limited by logistical burdens such as popular consent as much as irreconcilably contestable notions of the Good and those end-values which the law should be deemed to uphold.

Equity stands unique amongst legal subjects able to brave this dilemma by permitting such broad ethical principles as its maxims to furnish distinct solutions (albeit governed by historical rules dictating their proper application), both in terms of identifying the nature of wrongs suffered, and the specific means required of the court to rectify them. Such flexibility is unlikely to emerge in other fields, for a variety of reasons. To illustrate, criminal law requires widespread consistency and transparency so as to ensure the efficient alignment of police activity with court enforcement of due process. This is achieved often through strict liability offenses which disregard intention or other extenuating circumstances (on the legal substantive side) such that barristers are encouraged to preemptively seek guilty pleas per their own sober assessment of the unviability of their clients' cases, often with the view of achieving a commuted sentence (the procedural side), thereby freeing up court time to hear those trials with genuinely unpredictable outcomes. Turning to the civil side, commercial law generally requires certainty even at the cost of individual misfirings of justice so as to preserve the overall predictability of legal outcomes, allowing parties both to duly allocate risk where appropriate and to clearly assess their legal prospects accordant with established precedent, thereby often spurring settlement. Such practices increase the chances that neither the litigants nor courts are unnecessarily burdened by participating in cases whose outcomes should have prompted resolution before the litigation stage. Thus, it remains ideal that principles of construction, the timing and conditions under which terms are incorporated and vitiating factors of contracts all require unambiguous interpretation by jurists and laymen alike. Whereas other disciplines wield hammers, viewing every problem as a nail, equity's toolbox proves more varied. With its more specialized focus on areas which by their nature involve technicality and the unique fusion of notions of legal and beneficial ownership, equity has fashioned for itself a purview requiring attention to the specific subtleties of the case such that justice may be likelier done.

Following the Law

"Equity follows the law." This means principally two things: first, that equity will never act contrary to the black letter of common law; second, and more significantly, that its primary role is as a curative supplement to the deficiencies of the common law, *not* as a rival system. According to Benjamin Cardozo, Associate Justice of the US Supreme Court: "Equity works as a supplement for law and does not supersede the prevailing law."[1] The English legal historian Frederic William Maitland argued that law and equity served identical functions, albeit via different routes; equity was the recourse to the failure of the common law to provide effective remedy. Accordingly, in the absence of contrary evidence, the presumptions made by chancery courts are those determinable under the common law. Such presumptions acquire special importance in the context of co-ownership, the leading case of which is *Stack v Dowden* (2007).

The relevant facts are as follows. An unmarried couple purchased a house, legal title of which was under their joint names. They had cohabited for some eighteen years prior to acquiring this new property and between them had four children. The bulk of the purchase price was paid for by one party, Ms. Dowden, whilst subsequent mortgage payments were paid by both her and Mr. Stack. After some nine years, the relationship deteriorated, triggering Stack to seek a declaration that his former partner and he were tenants-in-common and that he was therefore entitled to a half-share in the proceeds of sale of the property. Though the High Court initially granted this, the decision was amended by the Court of Appeal, assigning a 65% share to Dowden and the remaining 35% to Stack. The House of Lords approved this ruling, citing that the parties had demonstrated the requisite intention to avoid the equitable presumption of co-equal beneficial ownership. The key behind their reasoning was the stringent separation of financial interests between both parties; throughout their cohabitation, each maintained a separate bank account from which the mortgage payments were made. This was sufficient to override the otherwise equitable presumption that when title to property is conveyed jointly (whereby legal co-ownership can only manifest itself via a joint tenancy), equitable ownership follows this division—that is, each of the parties shares 50% of the beneficial interest. Both parties had clearly demonstrated that they wished to resist the imposition

---

[1] *Graf v Hope Building Corporation* 254 N.Y 1 at 9 (1930)

of this presumption.

Accordingly, the ambit of equity in furnishing a remedy is circumscribed by the boundaries of the (common) law. Normally, Mr. Stack would have been entitled to a 50% share in the proceeds of sale, had it not been for the court's finding of an express contrary intention. This maxim sensibly recognizes the practical justice equity aims at achieving; that it cannot displace legal presumptions without destabilizing the administration of the judiciary, itself delicately balanced between two distinct traditions of law. For either to invade the jurisdiction of the other would be to diminish its authority and that of the edifice of law itself. A complicating factor is the lack of internal consensus regarding what the content *within* each legal system should be. For example, when assessing the scope of parties' intentions so as to assign beneficial shares under a constructive trust (as in this case), members of the House of Lords disagreed on the criteria to be applied; Baroness Hale advocated a multi-factorial approach inclusive of non-monetary considerations such as the domestic and familial nature of the parties' relationship. Lord Neuberger, issuing a strong dissent, alternatively argued that the inclusion of such factors would only inject woeful uncertainty into the determinations of the courts, thereby favoring reliance upon monetary expenditure. As he wrote, only "subsequent decisions, statements or actions, which can fairly be said to imply a positive intention to depart from that apportionment, will do to justify a change in the way in which the beneficial interest is owned."[1] By this he excluded the considerations taken into account by Baroness Hale, such as the rearing of children or any labors expended on the improvement of property (even those including financial expense) as a result of a loving relationship. Such internal infighting further renders the separation between the domains of law and equity paramount, such that neither reduces the efficacy of the other, especially so long as ongoing debates prevent finality as regards their treatment of those legal issues

---

1 [2007] 2 A.C. 432, [146]

which trigger their simultaneous and overlapping application. Moreover, the structure of equity cannot practically displace the binding legitimacy of either statutory law or furnish its own positive moral code. Not only are these constraints philosophical in nature owing to the illegitimacy of laws not obedient to the ultimate rule of recognition in English jurisprudence (*i.e.*, compliance with the legislature's will via the doctrine of parliamentary sovereignty), but administrative; no court, empowered to apply both law and equity, could function if the content of each conflicted and no hierarchy as to which branch should take priority was articulated.[1] Or, if the morality-based edicts of equity were to supersede the common law, then both systems would immediately lose all legitimacy; the former owing to the pervasive arbitrariness of individual judges' moral evaluations (thereby depriving the legal system of all predictability), the latter due to its express and constant overruling by equity. Rather, the *status quo* regarding the balance struck between the practical necessities of nomothetic principles being upheld—albeit imperfectly in certain individual cases—via the common law, and justice sensitive to particular litigants via equity, has been further refined in recent cases. *Jones v Kernott* (2011) expands the scope of *Stack v Dowden* to include an extended time frame in which parties could alter their erstwhile common intention regarding the assessment of respective beneficial shares, while the earlier case of *Oxley v Hiscock* (2004) allowed, in the absence of explicit agreement as to the size of a beneficial interest, its calculation to be based upon broad notions of fairness relative to the entire course of dealing between the parties. Both these cases demonstrate the premium placed upon the importance of ensuring each party receives his fair due. Meanwhile, the *Stack* presumption of equity following the law does not operate if title is not vested in joint names, or occurs in a non-domestic setting, per *Laskar v Laskar* (2008), decided the following year. Thusly,

---

1 Of course, we know that in such a conflict, equity prevails, though only because its disruption of the common law is relatively infrequent.

the demands of justice and commercial certainty are both broadly capable of simultaneous fulfillment under the present regime.

Hume's Guillotine

In his seminal *Treatise of Human Nature*, David Hume compellingly argues that what "is" does not necessarily dictate what "ought" to be. His argument proves a serious obstacle for natural lawyers attempting to divine from the laws of nature objective moral prescriptions. His guillotine, separating the descriptive from the prescriptive, is nevertheless overcome in equity, insofar as "equity looks on that as done that ought to be done." This is not to conflate what "is" legally as synonymous with what exists as part of the fundamental fabric of nature, but to create an avenue by which the former may facilitate a moral outcome per the momentum already set in motion by the preexisting legal scenario. For instance, a defect in procedure that has occurred shall not bar an equitable remedy which treats the prior state of affairs not as it happened, but as it should have happened. This approach was adopted in the landmark case of *Walsh v Lonsdale* (1882). A tenancy was issued, but without the necessary deed, rendering it equitable but not legal in nature. Nevertheless, the availability of specific performance rendered the equitable lease equivalent in function and indefeasibility to a legal one. The underpinning rationale is that as soon as the contract is entered, the vendor is transformed into a trustee, holding the property on behalf of the purchaser. Whereas the purchaser is entitled a proprietary interest, the vendor forfeits his in exchange for the cost of purchase.

The supplantation of legal reality within equitable prescription is among the more creative fixtures of equity and is the essence of its transformative power to rectify technical errors by substituting the noble fiction of their proper execution. In view of that, an overdue insurance payment, say, the result of a failed delivery owing to a processing error, may trigger the aforesaid maxim, where the alternative result would have been the entire forfeiture of the policy. Equity refashions the course of events to assume the correct procedure was followed in those cases where to not do so would yield a result which offends the conscience. This maxim requires great restraint in its application, not least for its potential to otherwise run roughshod over the requisite certainty and predictability of legal undertakings, especially contractual matters. That legal entitlement is still superior insofar as it binds the world, and its remedies are matters of right unlike the discretionary ones available via equity, should not be altered. These limitations on the potency of equity to interfere with the legal depiction of affairs are sensible in that they restrain its capacity for unregulated mischief. Instead, its sphere of action is, by virtue of its circumscription, better able to rectify injustice in the idiographic case without the imposition of sweeping reforms to the present law.

Equity as Equality

Like the aforesaid maxim, equity delights in equality. This is so not merely as guided by the principles of fair and just dealing between parties but as regards co-ownership of property, where equity, in the absence of contrary intention, assumes equal beneficial ownership shared between joint tenants. This maxim is usually triggered by the breakdown of a relationship requiring the court to divide up proprietary shares. Though preference is given to preserving the property whole, when partition is requested by a single party, equity is reluctant not to grant it. Such ensures that disagreement between landowners does not jeopardize the stable and efficient management of the property in question. The moral legitimacy of this maxim stems from the court's judicious handling of uncertainty. That is to say, the maxim is invoked regarding competing claims to ownership when the respective entitlement of either party is undocumented. The justness of equity intervenes to assign each one-half share (in the case of two claimants under a fixed trust, or an equally-divided share in the case of more than two).[1] This approach was extended in *Stack v Dowden* to apply between cohabiting partners, where there was no prior express declaration of the beneficial interests of either. Per Baroness Hale: "the starting point where there is joint legal ownership is joint beneficial ownership. The onus is upon the person seeking to show that the beneficial ownership is different from the legal ownership."[2] Such a conclusion is justified both on practical grounds (owing to evidentiary limitations insofar as reducing the laborious search for elusive evidence of a contrary intention) and the principled basis that neither party should benefit nor suffer in the presence of doubt, and should be treated impartially to the extent that recognition of their legal and beneficial equality permits.

Disavowing the Volunteer

It may appear at odds with the conscience-based jurisdiction of equity to deny relief to a volunteer. The very spirit of altruism on the part of this good Samaritan should be reflected in equity's ambition to reward—or at the very least not punish—such behavior. This maxim is opposed to such an aim, and for this reason is morally defective. However, before analyzing its faultiness, we must first attempt to understand its purported logic. That equity shall not assist a volunteer is taken to mean the denial of specific performance of a promise made in the absence of consideration. *Milroy v Lord* (1862) is authority for equity's reluctance to permit a beneficiary to benefit from an imperfectly-constituted trust failing the vesting of legal title in a trustee. In that case, this was so even in spite of the settlor's creation of a written deed and the provision of consideration for the shares he intended his niece to receive under the terms of the trust. The settlor's failure to transfer the shares to the intended trustee by way of company registration proved the crux of the matter in denying the forma-

---

1 *Burrough v Philcox* (1840), where the unspecified shares bequeathed to the testator's son and daughter were held equally between them.
2 [2007] 2 A.C. 454, [56]

tion of the trust, notwithstanding the unequivocal expression of the intentions of the former. That a court of equity cannot complete the transaction for want of this formality despite the presence of both clear intention *and* consideration arguably produces an unjust outcome.[1] This is especially so after the result in *Shah v Shah* (2010), whereby the Court of Appeal declared a valid trust where there too had been the incomplete transfer of shares. Perhaps most convincing is the judgment in *Pennington v Waine* (2002) in which the Court of Appeal held there were no rigid universal criteria in determining whether equity would assist a volunteer or perfect a faulty gift. The ultimate determining factor would be whether the absence of its construal would be unconscionable to the donee. This approach expands the "every effort doctrine" laid down in *Re Rose* and reflects a stronger willingness to enforce moral outcomes. Similar facts to *Milroy* existed in *Choithram International SA v Lalibai Thakurdas Pagarani* (2001), resulting in the Privy Council's judgment that for the donor to renege his gift would be unconscionable, considering the clarity of his intent to have previously done otherwise, and his having executed the appropriate deed. The court refused to set aside the gift, and to this extent, functionally assisted a volunteer.

Beyond the "every effort" rule, a further exception involves fortuitous vesting, in which a gift of property or the forgiveness of a debt is realized upon the donee acquiring legal title in said property. Additionally, considering that unconscionability may further create a trust (through the vehicle of proprietary estoppel) where one otherwise would not have existed, the current law would be more greatly unified with a generalized approach toward assisting a volunteer where there is sufficiently clear expression to do so, especially in the presence of consideration.

---

1 An exception to *Milroy v Lord* was articulated in *Re Rose* (1952), where a donor of a gift who takes all reasonable steps in his position to transfer the gift, subject to the default of a third party, may nevertheless have this failed legal transfer take effect in equity. This so-called 'every effort' doctrine should be extended to include situations such as arose in *Milroy*.

Criticism against the expansion of this maxim favors the perfected formalization of property transfer, at the cost of often ensuring practical justice inasmuch the settlor's intentions are both honored and shielded from rescindment. The ethical justification is twofold: to benefit the volunteer pursuant to his expectations following communication of the donor's will, and to prevent the latter resiling from his word.

In addition to the aforesaid, this maxim may be applied in an altogether different context in which it takes on a different meaning. Within the bourgeoning field of restitution, that equity will not aid a volunteer proves equally problematic in moral terms, but for different reasons from the above.[1] Whereas in the intentional transfer of property equity favors the rights of the current owner, as regards restitution, where property or improvement to it is mistakenly conveyed, equity will not aid an unwitting volunteer in its recovery.[2]

---

1 In restitution cases, the volunteer may be prevented from reclaiming a benefit already conferred to another party which failed to provide payment, whereas generally the issue which arises in relation to this maxim is the inadequacy of equity's enforcement of the expectations of a volunteer denied his bequest.

2 Restitution as an equitable remedy may however be trigged upon other wrongs being committed, namely that of unjust enrichment and, in particular, a breach of fiduciary duty. This is morally justified, considering the uniquely onerous burdens placed upon a trustee (say, relative to a generic tortious duty of care held between the operator of a motorcar and pedestrians), whereupon breach of his quasi-moral responsibilities to the beneficiary (such as violation of good faith and loyalty) demand severer punishment than the loss-based compensation favored by contract and tort. Accordingly, restitution permits the victim (*i.e.* the beneficiary) to recover the unauthorized gains made by his trustee via the breach (such as through improper investing of trust funds). It is fitting that restitution be used to measure damages in cases of breach of trust. As stated by Lord Browne-Wilkinson in *Target Holdings Ltd v Redferns* [1995] 3 All ER 793: 'the basic rule is that a trustee in breach of trust must restore or pay to the trust estate either the assets which have been lost to the estate by reason of the breach or compensation for such loss...Thus the common law rules of remoteness of damage and causation do not apply. However, there does have to be some causal connection between the breach of trust and the loss to the trust estate for which compensation is recoverable, viz. the fact that the loss would not have occurred but for the breach.' This influential case developed the principle that the assessment for compensation should be based upon the specific type of fiduciary duty breached. If a traditional trust,

That equity will not perfect an otherwise imperfect gift is a derivative maxim which does not require separate treatment. However, in addition to the abovementioned cases, the exception laid out in *Strong v Bird* (1874) signifies a retreat from the harshness of what is otherwise a maxim at odds with the spirit of equitable aims. So long as there is an unequivocal and on-going intention to forgive a debt up until the creditor's death, provided the debtor and executor are one and the same, he is released from his obligations. Greater moral force upholds the vigorous implementation of this maxim (under this narrow exception) insofar as there is no requirement of written evidence of the release of debt. There is a more contested expansion of this exception under the troublesome case of *Re Ralli's Will Trusts* (1964), which per its labyrinthine facts suggests broadening the creditor/debtor relationship beyond involving solely the settlor and donee, and that an ongoing intention to forgive the debt is not required. That this case should be considered dubious reveals the judicious restraint in applying this maxim, such that the absence of express intention, formality or concerted effort to perfect a gift ought to be interpreted so as to prevent the premature or unjust entanglement of the settlor vis-à-vis his embryonic promises.

The wide ambit of proprietary estoppel, however, firmly justified on grounds of principle, appears the final nail in the coffin regarding the legitimacy in continuing this maxim as it is presently applied, especially when considering the extensive inroads made by its numerous exceptions. The highest function of proprietary estoppel is to deny a party reliance upon his strict legal rights where to do so would produce an unjust outcome;

---

then restitution should be available. However, in a commercial transaction, as in the above case, the scale used to measure damages is comparable to the loss-based damages awarded under the common law. This is defensible owing to the nature of commercial transactions, where the invocation of equity is less pressing owing to a parity in resources and trade knowledge amongst commercial competitors (rather than in the conscience-based jurisdiction of equity which usually entails a bargaining position not held between equals).

this often overlaps with the court's perfection of an otherwise defective transfer of property. The court has a nearly limitless discretion in the assignment of an equitable entitlement to the injured party, taking into account such factors as the overall nature of their past dealings, the magnitude of the moral breach and the outstanding rights which may be adversely affected by third parties. This is lauded, for whilst such free rein might be discouraged owing to the unique ills and interests which must be prevented and protected, respectively, in other areas of law, equity alone has the charge of alleviating the law of its nomothetic rigidity, opening up the possibility of flexibility subsequent to its creative resolution of unique injustices. However, the court's quest for a fair conclusion ensures that it abides by the principle of proportionality, such that the defendant is not unduly punished if his infractions have been minor. Where his actions have incurred detrimental reliance falling short of egregious harm done to the claimant, the court will flex the muscles of equity in the latter's favor such that monetary damages, rather than exclusively equitable remedies (such as transfer of proprietary ownership, considered a more prized outcome because of the uniqueness of land), shall be conferred; such was the case in the previously discussed *Jennings v Rice* (2002), where in spite of the representations made to the claimant that he would receive his former employer's house in Somerset, he was instead awarded the cash sum of £200,000, the Court of Appeal upholding the High Court's assessment as a fair one under the circumstances.

Nothing in Vain

Despite the emphasis equity places upon creative solutions otherwise not conceived by the common law, there is a limit to its capacity to provide redress. In fact, it is equity's very concern with supplying a practicable resolution that discourages a court from implementing any of the aforesaid maxims *en route* toward providing an equitable remedy only to have it weakened or nullified by another piece of legal machinery.[1] For instance, a court will not grant rectification of a contract if specific performance will thereafter not be provided upon the revised terms. Owing to the moral exceptionalism of equitable remedies, this maxim proves a limiting factor curtailing the extent the common law will be overridden. This is highly advisable considering that every intrusion by equity further disrupts the certainty and universality of the common law; such interference should not be permitted except where a principled justification to do so exists and where that principled basis may be enforced. Otherwise, the moral ambition of equity is stultified and the force of the common law needlessly diminished.

The corollary of this maxim is that whenever an equitable remedy may be viably implemented, equity will provide its aid to the furthest possible extent—occasionally expressed in the phrase that "equity will not do justice by halves." Accordingly, a claimant's successful application for equitable relief does not bar his simultaneous entitlement to common law damages, an outcome made all the more accessible by virtue of the court's dual jurisdiction to enforce both types of relief.

---

1 'Equity will do nothing in vain.' *Jones v Lipman* [1962] 1 All ER 442

PART II: PERFECTING EQUITY

CHAPTER IV: REFORM

THUS FAR, much of our time has been spent examining what the current state of equity is and offering a moral analysis of its justness. Unlike other areas of law, swayed more by logistical and policy considerations, such an undertaking is uniquely relevant to the future of equity, owing to its intended alignment of the rigors of the common law with the application of moral principles toward the relief of individual claimants. We shall move a step beyond academic criticism to supply practical steps which may be taken in the future development of this area of law. Naturally, not every conceivable improvement desired is practicable, and accordingly our focus here shall be on some of the more pressing defects at present. Before we begin, it behooves us to take a step back and examine the edifice of this unique branch of law. Every other legal discipline has at its core a corpus of statutes or cases (and in the rarer case of constitutional law, also a set of foundational documents and conventions) which help develop its guiding principles. No doubt ethical considerations inform and shape the character of subsequent generations of these fields, influenced by changing social mores and what appears to be an ever-increasing respect for individual rights and a decline in the judicial enforcement of communitarian morals. Equity, however, operates in reverse; founded as the last bastion in which practical justice was achievable in an otherwise inadequate legal system, it proceeded on the basis of general moral principles which themselves evolved into their own semi-rigid framework of rules, remedies, recognized rights and jurisdiction.

No area of the law is immune to consolidation or rationalization, and these inevitable processes have had a mixed effect upon the original aims first pursued by the Court of Chancery. Whilst the formalization of equity as a distinct species of law has galvanized its legitimacy in preserving the rights of property owners and their dependents, so too has it required the eternal vigilance of any entrepreneur, representative or mere settlor in the dealing of his assets when impactful upon third parties. The increasing formality of equity therefore both enshrines and limits the effectiveness of the moral principles upon which it was founded, no doubt owing to the perennial tension between requiring a flexible sensibility in the treatment of novel factual scenarios so as to promote a bespoke and evenhanded judgment, and the necessity of ensuring a minimal degree of predictability and consistency to the law, thereby occasionally turning a blind eye to unique circumstances of distress whose remedy would come as the unraveling of a set of legal principles whose efficacy is derived from their uniform constancy.

Before continuing to address our specific grievances, it is fitting to first ask a broader question: what is the ultimate function of law? Whilst we delved into a wider jurisprudential critique of its entire nature (not confined to the domain of equity) at this book's beginning, a second glance is helpful in refining our understanding of both its eventual objective and the means it employs toward securing that end. Law, first and foremost, seeks the establishment of social order. This is required as the prerequisite to all subsequent human flourishing. If we take happiness, both individual and collective, as the ultimate aim of man, then we recognize the inability to pursue this aim so long as we live in a Hobbesian state of nature that necessarily views human interaction as predicated upon conflict, rather than consensus; the blunt nature of law appears to robustly support this thesis. For in the absence of law, none of us can be confident in the continued civil behavior of our fellow citizens. Without order, fear amongst even the gentlest would run amok owing to their destructive distrust of their fellow man. The fear in man's ever-present suspicion of his brothers and their selfish motives is neutralized by the impartial submission required of us all to the State and its edicts. Ultimately, respect for its institutions is only possible under the threat of force.

Those moral ambitions held by the law, such as epitomized under equity, which attempt to elevate this discipline from a blunt instrument of pacifying oppression to one in which the *bona fide* content of justice is imbued in the hearts of men, must be recognized as a necessarily derivative, and elitist, aim: derivative because the facilitation of ethical behavior amongst the citizenry can only occur in the presence of stability (*i.e.,* the maintenance of social order), and elitist because the promotion of particular ethical ideals will always be a contested undertaking in which those closest to the legislative and judicial apparatuses of the State will have the greatest clout. To this extent, there is a necessary and ineradicable gulf between the aspirations of morality and law. Whereas the former is centrally concerned with an individual's just entitlement to happiness, and thus his psychological prosperity, the latter regulates the behavior of competing and often insatiable interests, requiring that the means employed to pursue them abide by a common normative guideline. This minimal standard is usually expressed as justice, which is most convincingly defined as hedonic reciprocity—the balancing of the utile magnitudes between the actions of two or more parties. Thus, the law is more concerned with preventing the exploitation of others than with the promotion of a positive duty to care for one's fellow man. Law must cater to the great multitude, therefore serving the interests of the least necessarily evil man amongst us.

Individual statutes and the precedential gravity of *rationes decidendi* are therefore instances of rule utilitarianism, so deemed not only because they do not capture an innate moral truth beyond the instrumental maximization of utility (herein best understood pursuant to the preservation of social order), but because they may be overridden in times of crisis. The immutable majesty of the law is hardly so under exceptional circumstances; conscription in the face of war, heightened taxation in the midst of economic depression, infringement of individual privacy in the name (genuine or not) of upholding national security—are all major departures from the "rights" we, as citizens, assume are both inviolable and essential in maintaining the legitimacy of our sociopolitical order. For, if the welfare of its people is not respected, what justification does the government possess to continue its rule? Accordingly, the divorce between ethics and law must be recognized as one based upon their respective aims, which are not mutually exclusive but rather occasionally intersect. Moral duty is objective and non-negotiable; law necessitates compromise. An ethical imperative binds all actors in all situations; extenuating circumstances may excuse an otherwise culpable party just as strict liability may punish a blameless one. The moral infusion of law is only possible following its success in quelling social unrest; once this primary and original goal is achieved the shaping of civic conscience at large may be attempted, but only insofar as the bounds of cultural tolerability and the very limits of our human nature permit. That is to say, law can never successfully reengineer our psyche to abandon selfish impulse for the nobler goal of communitarian sacrifice, much as the legalization of practices hitherto considered taboo cannot occur suddenly and without widespread public approval. Whereas morality is independent of individual perspective, the survival of law vitally depends upon mass approval, for, in its absence, social solidarity breaks down and so too the enforceability of law (short of brutish, militaristic means, themselves liable to trigger revolutionary activity fatal to the maintenance of the social order required not only for the continuation of the rule of law itself, but which constitutes the very stasis law seeks to preserve under normal conditions).

Evolving moral sensibilities have no doubt improved and made more just the content of law, but these can principally be explained in terms of their enhancement of individual self-interest, rather than enforcement of potent community-oriented norms. For instance, the decriminalization of homosexuality could be understood as an ethical step forward not because it loosened its grip upon the enforcement of social morality, but because it liberated *individuals* to pursue their private life without fear of legal recrimination. Such sexual freedom is ultimately predicated upon a Millian understanding of rights not as necessarily socially approved, but as self-regarding acts which, by virtue of their lacked (adverse) impact on others, ought to be immune from the proselytizing oversight of the state and even prevailing cultural norms. Duly, the moral content of law, however refined from the basest non-aggression principles first articulated at the dawn of social organization, cannot exceed the perception shared amongst individual members of a community that it serves their best interests, even if that translates into yielding suboptimal net collective utility. Individuals conform to the social contract precisely because it provides a richer, more secure lifestyle than otherwise possible; for the law to disregard the incentive which ensures its compliance—that is, the public belief that its aims align with optimally satisfying the interests of those who obey it—would be to effectively sign its own death warrant.

Utility maximization is therefore the highest goal of law, achieved through a variety of means, commencing with the preservation of social order. Only in the context of a stable framework in which interdependence is facilitated may any opportunity for collective gain exist. Beyond this initial point, however, utility is best served through the maximization of individual in-terest, and toward this end, law essentially becomes a means of ensuring the just distribution of goods, so deemed per the utile desert of any given party. Justice in the legal sense, as informed by utilitarian consideration, translates into upholding both physical and economic factors. The former is exhibited through the law's obvious concern with preserving bodily integrity. The utile justification for punishing an offender who commits rape or aggravated battery is the unwarranted violation of the vic-tim's bodily integrity, unwarranted because the harm inflicted was not in due response to a similar violation (or performed for a beneficial purpose, such as surgery) as suffered by the crimi-nal and caused by the victim. The law therefore becomes the avenger of infringements of victims' rights, and, whilst not so exacting as to inflict a qualitatively identical punishment as the harm caused by the offender (*e.g.*, raping a rapist or executing a murderer [in non-death penalty jurisdictions]), ensures that he must suffer for his infractions through the forfeiture of his personal liberties. Economic justice is upheld through the law of contract; a promise becomes legally binding insofar as it affects one's financial standing, whereby such an agreement conforms to the prior requirements of contractual obligation (*viz.* formal offer and acceptance, consideration, requisite certainty of terms, intention to be legally bound). Modern legislation, such as the UK's Unfair Contract Terms Act 1977 and Unfair Terms in Con-sumer Contracts Regulations 1999 in particular, have ventured further to provide consumers (the relatively weaker bargaining party in a commercial transaction) the legally enforceable right to ensure that the agreements they undertake are fundamentally fair in nature, though important exceptions continue to apply (such as the law's forced ignorance to evaluating the adequacy of subject matter or consideration of the bargain).

Altogether, the law's delicate balance between protecting the physical and economic welfare of individual citizens while simultaneously ensuring collective stability overall, adeptly maximizes utility at both the local and global level, creating a framework in which individual desert is preserved whilst concurrently seeking the common good. Whilst equity favors the former aim, it gracefully fulfills both functions with a high degree of efficacy owing to its marked deference to the relatively-universalized system of the common law (a deference made all the more admirable considering that when the two bodies of law conflict, it is equity which prevails). That equity is therefore sensitive to the limited nature of its applicability ensures that the law is not so saturated with moralism as to not readily translate into good policy, such that it may continue to function as a forum in which predictability and uniformity preserve public faith in its capacity to deal swiftly and aggressively with habitual infractions.

All of this is to further emphasize the uniqueness of equity law—that branch principally concerned not with social pacification or appeasement but rather the enforcement of substantive morals via the bureaucracy of the judiciary, its jurisdiction systemically institutionalized to include every court of law able to hear before it a common law grievance. Such was the noble genius of the Judicature Acts—to provide equitable relief subsequent to even the minutest failing of the case-based jurisprudence upon which was traditionally relied. Nonetheless, we cannot expect moral faultlessness (not least owing to the aforesaid limitations of the entirety of law itself in upholding ethical precepts) in light of the fact that every social institution constructed by man is to be contaminated in the reflection of his flaws.

Nevertheless, what follows shall be our humble attempt to ever-perfect a system incapable of perfection. How the aforementioned maxims may be more faithfully and efficiently applied as they relate to particular substantive features of equity—such as tracing and the unique remedies it provides—shall be discussed. Whilst we concede that as a legal discipline equity excels both in the philosophical purity of its aims and the vigor with which it is able to implement them, progress remains to be made. Consider such an exercise not futile owing to our inextinguishable capacity for asymptotic improvement, and our endless need for activity in the face of injustice, however great or small. We shall begin with an ever-increasingly anachronistic instrument of equity: advancement under a resulting trust.

Advancement

The logic behind a resulting trust operates from the premise that equity "assumes bargains, not gifts." This means that in the absence of contrary intention, equity astutely recognizes that the provision of money toward the purchase of property morally requires the provider of money to acquire an interest in said property, even where legal title is vested exclusively in a copurchaser or one who provided none of his own funds, instead receiving them entirely from the otherwise-legally unrecognized donor. Equity intervenes to ensure that a trust results on behalf of the donor, to the extent of his financial contribution. A resulting trust operates by law, not the settlor's intentions (this is less true in the case of an attempt made by a settlor to create a trust, but where for any number of reasons it fails to be properly created).[1] This is known as a presumed intention resulting trust, though it can also occur where there is a voluntary transfer of land (unlike in a situation where a donor provides money to purchase a new property, the donor here transfers title to another person so as to make its receipt resemble a gift). Such was the case in *Hodgson v Marks* (1971), where a homeowner transferred title to a lodger on the understanding that she would retain the beneficial interest in the property. When the lodger reneged on this agreement, selling the property to a third party, her beneficial interest was triggered, binding the purchaser. The resulting

---

1 Per Lord Browne-Wilkinson in *Westdeutsche Landesbank v Islington LBC* (1996), a resulting trust can form automatically pursuant to a failure to create a valid trust in regard to its technical formation, including defective declaration, lack of a specified purpose and there remaining an unexhausted beneficial interest.

trust is falling out of favor, and the role of the constructive trust has since become more prominent because of its relatively unrestricted ambit to provide practical justice, unconstrained by arithmetic calculations of financial contribution as translated into proprietary interest. Instead, it is able to calculate beneficial shares taking into account the whole course of dealings between the parties and the nature of their relationship, potentially irrespective of direct financial matters.[1]

Advancement comes to the fore when there is a sufficient counter-presumption that a direct financial contribution or voluntary transfer of property should *not* trigger the law's creation of a resulting trust. The underpinning rationale is that there are certain circumstances in which the transferor has a natural desire or obligation to provide for the transferee, namely, in the case of the voluntary conveyance of property between a husband and his wife[2] or a father and his child.[3] At first glance, this may appear an appropriate exception considering the strong familial bonds which often motivate such charity on the part of the transferor. However, it is the discriminatory application of the principle of advancement which renders it contrary to the modern incarnation of equitable precepts insofar as they seek unbiased justice. For instance, in the eyes of the law a mother possesses no similar duty as a father in caring for her child, such that the presumption of a gift will not arise[4] in the event she conveys property to her offspring. Equally, if a wife were to transfer property in the name of her husband, advancement would not apply. The principal defect of advancement is its antiquated gender bias, which strikes against the very heart of equity's assurance of fair dealing between all parties. Of course, it is only a presumption, and accordingly may be rebutted by sufficient evidence, as was successfully done in *Warrent v Gurney* (1944), where a father's re-

---

1 As determined in *Oxley v Hiscock* (2004).
2 *Silver v Silver* (1958)
3 *Dyer v Dyer* (1788)
4 *Bennet v Bennet* (1879)

tention of the deeds to a house he purchased and conveyed to his daughter was held adequate proof of his desire not to provide the property to her as an apparent gift. However, the fact that the presumption remains to be overcome is unavoidably problematic in this day and age. Calls for reform have proven hitherto ineffectual: s.199 of the Equality Act 2010 intended to abolish advancement, though it remains not yet in force. Not only does the current law offend the holistic objective of equity, but may in fact run explicitly contrary to international law as a violation of Article 5, Seventh Protocol to the European Convention on Human Rights, which requires equality between spouses.

Abolishing Exoneration Clauses

It is not uncommon for the trust document to include clauses limiting or outright excluding the liability of trustees subsequent to breach of their fiduciary duties. This exclusion cannot reach so far as to hold harmless a trustee in the case of fraud or dishonest conduct.[1] This last caveat is not unproblematic. Fraud and dishonesty are considered difficult to characterize, especially in the ill-suited confines of the chancery courts. Accordingly, a quasi-criminal standard has been invoked, whereby dishonest conduct on the part of the trustee is determined in reference to whether a) the ordinary man would deem it so (the objective test) and b) the trustee himself was aware of this standard (the subjective test).[2] Unfortunately, this standard appears less viable when applied in a civil setting which bars the presence of a jury, whose members can more readily apply their own considerations of proper conduct in the determination of the "ordinary" regard of honest behavior than a judge accustomed to legal guidelines for evidentiary discovery rather than quotidian benchmarks.

However, the true crux of the matter is not so much the finer

1 *Baker v JE Clark & Co (Transport) Ltd* (2006). Moreover, where the breach of trust is fraudulent, the limitation period does not apply: Limitation Act 1980, s.21(1)(a).
2 *Cavell USA Ltd v Seaton Insurance Company* (2009)

points of excluding fraud from the ambit of trustee liability, but rather the extent to which non-fraudulent behavior itself should be protected. The nature of a trustee distinguishes his actions from other legal (and non-legal) undertakings, such that the duty of care thrust upon him is higher relative to the common man. This higher duty extends beyond his mere professional expertise, in fact elevating it above the standard required of similar professionals in their own fields (*e.g.*, solicitors, medical practitioners, etc.). This is because of the moral responsibility inherent in the trustee's duty, which encompasses more than mere vocational diligence. His equitable relationship to the beneficiary is centrally concerned with upholding obligations of good faith and unconditional loyalty. The law has accordingly subtly transformed his duty from being strictly legal to semi-moral, albeit legally enforceable. Duly, the very idea of any clause seeking to limit, let alone exclude, fault-based liability appears antithetical to the unique and onerous burdens equity places upon the trustee. Accordingly, the current law is unsatisfactory, despite being recently reaffirmed in *Barraclough v Mell* (2005). Here, the High Court ruled that a trustee's exemption clause was valid despite the trustee having misdirected over £60,000 to the wrong beneficiaries! The specific clause excluded liability for negligence and was upheld.

The sum total of the erosion of fiduciary liability is the gradual emasculation of equity's power to protect the interests of the beneficiary. This trend is unambiguously disconcerting, and one which must be corrected so as to preserve the moral force of this branch of law. It is obviously agreed that trustee liability should not be excluded for fraudulent or dishonest behavior, but nor should immunity extend to include negligence or any other fault-based breach of prescribed duty. The result is detriment to the beneficiary, despite suggestions that this may be avoided if professional trustees were required to be insured against liability. Whilst this would ameliorate the situation, the root of the problem is the legal enforceability of overly expansive exemption clauses. Ending their reign was seriously considered by a 2003 proposal of the Law Commission, though lamentably it was rejected three years later in their Report, "Trustee Exemption Clauses." Pressure from practitioners forced the commission's adoption of a half-way (and unacceptable) measure whereby trustees were strongly recommended (though again, not required) to explain in full the meaning and extent of their potential exclusion of liability to beneficiaries upon the creation of a trust.

Tracing the Labyrinth

Tracing is an indispensable weapon in the arsenal of equity to combat the exploitation of beneficial interests. It is triggered when the proceeds of a breach of trust are received by a third party, either via the processes of *following* or *tracing*. The former refers to the identification of trust property whose unauthorized transfer did not alter its original form; for instance, trust money being deposited in the bank account of the transferee which had a prior balance of zero (thereby creating no problems as regarding the ownership of the money sent). Tracing is invoked upon the thornier instance of the transfer of property whose form has been altered in some way (trust funds being used to purchase stock shares, etc.), whether in itself or by virtue of amalgamation with other, unfungible property (the best example being other funds) actually owned by the third party.

Despite the potency of this procedure (tracing is considered neither a bona fide right nor remedy), such as its capacity to reclaim the beneficiary's proprietary interest in trust assets even when transferred to a complicit third party subsequent to the trustee's bankruptcy, its implementation is unnecessarily complicated, such that its substantive aims are often unduly fettered. This is largely because different sets of byzantine rules govern tracing in common law and at equity. Criticism of this state of affairs is not in short supply, and well summarized by no less a figure than Millett LJ (now Lord Millett) in *Jones (FC) &*

Sons v Jones (1996), who cited his discontent with the unmeritorious distinction "given that tracing is neither a right nor a remedy but merely the process by which the plaintiff establishes what has happened to his property and makes good his claim that the assets which he claims can properly be regarded as representing his property."[1] Despite these calls for reform, the law has remained unchanged, as confirmed in the 2003 case of *Shalson v Russo*.

Unification of the tracing rules is recommended, favoring the approach taken by equity, not least because it allows for the more convoluted transfer of trust property than under the common law, whereby tracing misappropriated funds is limited to the extent it is not mixed with other property. Particular regard should be paid to two hitherto failed attempts by those advocating the expansion of the ambit of equitable relief via the *swollen assets* and *backwards tracing* theories. The former suggests that the general assets of the wrongdoer should be vulnerable once the beneficiary's assets can no longer be distinctly located, such as upon the third party's receipt of trust funds paid into an overdrawn account, but where he possesses other accounts with positive balances. Per viewing the sum total of the defendant's assets as having "swelled" following receipt of unauthorized funds, the claimant ought to be allowed to deduct his misappropriated assets from the non-overdrawn accounts. This approach has been rejected thus far, as in *Serious Fraud Office v Lexi Holdings Plc* (2009). Similar is equity's appeal to the specific culpable intentions of the wrongdoer per the *backwards tracing* theory. This applies where an asset acquired prior to breach of trust though intended to be financed via the later misappropriation of such funds is not immune from the jurisdiction of the courts, which may backdate the breach of trust to coincide with the invalid acquisition of property. Despite the justness of this approach, it too has been disapproved in *Bishopsgate Investment Management v Homan* (1995).

---

1 [1996] 3 W.L.R. 703

Both of these approaches afford the beneficiary the practical means to enforce his proprietary interest, while offending neither public policy nor the proprietary rights of a third party, considering that such tracing could only occur following confirmation of misappropriation of funds and the identity of their recipient. That a remedy may be denied once the funds are exhausted is unsatisfactory where additional means—unconnected to the specific transaction but available per the defendant's general property—are available. Such modest reforms to the current law would not disrupt the soundness of the other limitations imposed regarding the scope of tracing, such as where no proprietary claim may be pursued against a *bona fide* purchaser without notice for value (alternatively known as equity's darling)[1] or where a claimant will be barred relief if he comes to court without clean hands. More problematic becomes the issue of recovering exhausted trust funds from an innocent, albeit unentitled, recipient where to do so would cause an injustice against him. This was the knotty poser encountered by the Court of Appeal in *Re Diplock* (1948). The relevant facts included that the testator's residuary estate had been improperly distributed to a number of charities (nor was the gift exclusively charitable, as is required under the Charities Act 2011); however, this went undiscovered until the exhaustion of funds in one case whereby a charity paid off its loans. Where the testator's funds had not been mixed, these were rightly held on trust for the beneficiaries (the next of kin), but as regards those monies used to pay off debts and expended on the erection of buildings, the court ruled that such funds could not be disentangled for the benefit of the next of kin, not least because of the financial detriment which would be incurred by the charity representing an innocent volunteer. This much of the ruling appears ethically sound, although we question the degree of "financial integration" required on the part of the volunteer before the funds received are no longer recover-

---

1 As per the ruling in *Sinclair Investments (UK) Ltd v Versailles Trade Finance Ltd* (2011).

able by the rightful beneficiaries. Should expenditure on a building project truly suffice, or should such property simply be sold and the money held on trust for the beneficiaries? Of course, this must be balanced with the reasonable expectation which must be enforced by the courts to impose temporal limitations upon the claims brought by beneficiaries whereby those third parties in receipt of trust property do so without the taint of dishonesty, and must be assumed to transform into the rightful owners eventually. This mirrors the practical logic of both the equitable maxim that equity assists only the vigilant and the provision for adverse possession in land law. Property is ultimately a power relationship recognized in reality, of which the law conforms to accept. Nonetheless, it is suggested that where the value of funds used even toward the alteration and acquisition of different types of property may be identified, so long as economic injustice (rather than logistical inconvenience) does not result to the third party, beneficial requisition should still be available within a reasonable time frame, the latter being a question of fact per the unique circumstances of the case.

A last and particularly inadequate feature of current tracing rules involves the reluctance of courts to access funds per the lowest intermediate balance rule. Here, assume that the trustee has £10,000 in his account misappropriated from the trust. He spends £8,000, reducing the balance to £2,000, later depositing £5,000 of his own money. This raises his balance to £7,000. The beneficiary will only be entitled to access the original £2,000, and *not* any of the subsequent £5,000 the trustee has deposited. The rationale is that the original trust property can no longer be identified, despite the wrongful intentions of the trustee being sufficiently evidenced for tracing to bite. This was the unsatisfactory result of *Bishopsgate v Homan* (1995), which also held that money paid into an overdrawn bank account is treated as lost for the purposes of beneficial recovery. This stands as one of the more egregious perversions of a fair outcome being achievable at equity owing to the intrusion of unjust rules hampering an effective remedy for the claimant. So long as the assets of the trustee are not transferred to an innocent third party (barring the qualifications aforementioned), they should be accessible by the beneficiary following proof of misappropriation. The overdrawn exclusion is sound insofar as a bank whose debt has been discharged should not be held responsible for the breaches of its client; however, if the beneficiary were permitted to access the misallocated funds deposited into an overdrawn account which rendered its balance positive again, no greater injustice would be done, for either the beneficiary or the bank will suffer in this situation. That the bank has greater resources at its disposal, and may seek a personal action against the trustee for the overdrawn funds, is a proposal arguably more sensitive to the hardship caused to the beneficiary than a large financial institution (although again, the beneficiary is a volunteer who furnished no consideration, unlike the bank).[1]

Formalities Concerning Disposition of an Equitable Interest

Section 53(1)(c) of the Law of Property Act 1925 has caused considerable confusion due to both textual ambiguity and subsequent interpretation in case law, the latter owing to the ulterior motives of tax avoidance usually present as regards what qualifies as a disposition rather than declaration of trust. Before critically examining case law and potential reform, let us first turn to the provision which deals overall with those instruments required to be in writing:

---

1 That the bank should seek a personal action against the trustee is justified insofar as the beneficiary has such rights as regards one who has provided dishonest assistance toward the misappropriation of trust property, even if he has not retained any of it for himself. Such an individual may still be personally liable to compensate the beneficiary for the loss suffered by the trust. This liability stands so long as the third party engaged in dishonest assistance, even if the trustee himself was not acting dishonesty. The test for dishonesty was laid out in *Twinsectra Ltd v Yardley* (2002), whereby the House of Lords advanced a hybrid classification based upon subjective guilt and the objective assessment of dishonest behavior. The objective element was considered sufficient however, in the later case of *Barlow Clowes International Ltd (In Liquidation) v Eurotrust International Ltd* (2006).

A disposition of an equitable interest or trust sub-sisting at the time of the disposition, must be in writing signed by the person disposing of the same or by his agent thereunto lawfully authorized in writing or by will.

Of course, as clarified in section 53(2), this section is irrelevant as regards the creation and operation of resulting, implied and constructive trusts, as such are often constructed informally and designed to prevent what would, in the face of unyielding requirements for statutory formality, be an unjust outcome. To require their compliance with the above provision would be contrary to their very purpose. Returning to the section, it must be noted that it applies *following* the creation of a trust and not its declaration which first gives rise to an equitable interest. It is of relevance only upon the transfer of such equitable interest in the settlor's property (which may include chattels in addition to land). However, there is ambiguity as regards what constitutes a declaration of trust as opposed to the disposition of an equitable interest. The difference is significant because the latter may attract a stamp duty, unlike the declaration of the trust itself. Therefore, whereas the Inland Revenue Service favors construing any doubt in favor of the existence of a disposition, it is to the settlor's advantage to declare a trust which shields tax being levied on the actual transaction. Considering the tax consequences may be substantial (especially the larger the trust), greater clarity in this area of law is needed.

The first two cases we must consider are *Grey v Inland Revenue Commissioners* and *Oughtred v IRC*, both from 1960. In the former, the issue was whether a settlor could adequately communicate to his trustees via an oral request to have shares transferred to third party beneficiaries or whether subsequent written confirmation on their part was necessary, thereby creating an equitable disposition. The House of Lords held the latter, as oral instructions could not suffice to transfer the shares in question.

Stamp duty was therefore attracted. In *Oughtred*, the House of Lords were forced to classify a formal transfer of shares (though pursuant to an oral agreement) under section 53(1)(c). Again, they held that an equitable disposition existed, thereby incurring stamp duty. This reasoning is less convincing than in *Grey*, because in the present case it was argued that a constructive subtrust was created whereby the equitable interest was transferred prior to documentary (in this case, contractual) exchange. This was particular to the facts of the case, whereby a son had orally agreed to transfer his interest in remainder to his mother, and contended that the disposition therefore occurred independently of the formation of a written contract. The House of Lords rejected this argument.[1] A third and final case to assess is the infamous *Vandervell v IRC* (1967), so noted for its peculiar complexity regarding the longevity of an option to retain an equitable interest. Its peculiar facts aside, the House of Lords ruled that the oral instructions of a beneficiary under a bare trust directing his trustees to transfer legal and equitable interest to a third party shall be honored by the courts. This portion of the judgment appears sound, though less so in its support for the argument advanced by the Inland Revenue claiming that the appellant did not fully divest himself of his equitable interest despite the vesting of legal title in trustees, thereby incurring a substantial stamp duty. Our truest discontent with the current law, however, emerges in a derivative case the following decade, *Re Vandervell Trusts (No. 2)* (1974), where the eponymous appellant sought to finally divest himself of any lingering equitable interest potentially held in shares bequeathed to his children via a trust corporation he established. Despite executing a deed of release which expressly transferred his equitable interest in shares to his trust company for the benefit of his children, the

---

1 It is generally thought that a subtrust in which the entire beneficial interest is not transferred constitutes an exception to s.53(1)(c); however, as the entire interest was transferred in this case, it was held that this required a written transfer, and that therefore the contract served as vital to the disposition of the equitable interest.

Inland Revenue claimed tax on the dividends that had been paid on those shares for part of the intervening period. This was because three years elapsed between the ruling in *Vandervell v IRC* and Vandervell's express transfer of equitable interest. The Inland Revenue claimed significant tax on the dividends yielded during this period, amounting to over £750,000. The Court of Appeal held that a valid declaration of trust had been made, thereby shielding the trust from further tax liability (overturning the decision by Megarry J in the High Court).

While the decision may have produced a just outcome, it is problematic for multiple reasons. First, it is implausible that a trust corporation operating as a trustee could functionally create a declaration of trust, as implicitly required in the Court's judgment. Second, the equitable transfer of Vandevell's interest in the shares to his children appears more like a disposition than an outright declaration of trust, especially as facilitated through his trust corporation which implies that the trust was already in existence, thereby engaging section 53(1)(c). Third concerns the lengthy judgment of Lord Denning in which he claims that per the circumstances of *No. 2*, had Vandervell retained his post-option interest in the shares, then he would have been estopped from reclaiming it once transferred to his children. This is unlikely, because the initiation of estoppel is designed to prevent manifestly unconscionable outcomes and not the sort which might have arisen under these circumstances—that is, whatever amount the children may have been forced to refund to their father if he insisted on his post-option rights, in light of the fact that they just received a massive inheritance (hardly the sort of detriment estoppel should be preoccupied with correcting). Notwithstanding this unlikelihood, should estoppel arise, it is correct that it may do so in light of the spirit of s.53(2) without the need for writing, as was confirmed in *Singh v Anand* (2008), where a one-third share in a company was awarded following a promise to that effect (in the absence of written formalities).

Unexhausted Beneficial Interest

There are multiple grounds upon which a trust may fail, including an unexhausted beneficial interest. In such an event, a variety of theories exists as to how the surplus assets should be allocated. These include the presumption that a resulting trust arises, as suggested in *Re Printers and Transferrers Amalgamated Trades Protection Society* (1899), where a surplus of funds was held on resulting trust for society members and distributed amongst them relative to their previous contributions. This was echoed in *Re Hobourn Aero Components Limited's Air Raid Disaster Fund* (1946), whereby any contributor to a charitable undertaking could recover his money if the purpose of the fund was fully executed, leaving a surplus held on resulting trust for the donor(s). The fact that this approach has become unfashionable is unfortunate.

An alternative is *bona vacantia*, whereby surplus funds are directed to the Crown.[1] Despite the natural aversion of unclaimed funds ultimately being acquired by the government (as opposed to an arguably worthier recipient, such as any one of a list of pre-approved charities), there is an irreducible logic that upon the exhaustion of beneficiaries, the government is the impartial receptacle with the best claim to whatever interest remains, owing to its principal role as tax collector and its generic entitlement to whatever property is not held specifically by individual citizens.[2]

---

1 Per *Cunnack v Edwards* (1895). Here, a society was dissolved which had formerly provided annuity payments to the widows of former members. Despite all such persons having been paid, a surplus existed, and it was stipulated that this belonged to the Crown. This theory is favored where all members of a society are deceased (*Re Bucks Constabulary Fund (No. 2)* (1979), although its operation may be displaced by a single survivor. This was the case in *Hanchett-Stamford v AG* (2006), where absolute entitlement was justified under the contract-holding theory. In brief, it states that the distribution of assets is in accordance with the contractual principles agreed upon by the members themselves. In their absence, an equal division is assumed.

2 Such as under the ancient allodial right to property ownership which historically assigned all property to the ruling monarch, a privilege now diluted to the constitutional government.

However, there are limits as to how far this principle should be applied, as evidenced in the unsatisfactory case of *Davis v Richards and Wallington Industries Ltd* (1990). Here, Scott J ruled that employers' overpayments to a pension fund could be refundable under a resulting trust, astutely recognizing that the mere exhaustion of a beneficial interest should not disqualify its creation (by operation of law). Less satisfactory is that employees' contributions would be received by the Crown as *bona vacantia*, so argued because no straightforward means of apportionment could be devised amongst the wide class of employees. This is unacceptable reasoning on two grounds; firstly, unlike in a moribund society whose members have all died (thereby leaving no potential beneficiaries), live beneficiaries can be ascertained and they alone should benefit from the distribution of assets. Secondly, logistical difficulty in determining entitlement is less relevant as an obstacle than is an undeserved windfall enjoyed by the government, not least because it offends the principle of justice. Whereas employee contributors were the source of such funds, it is not equitable that the fruits of their labor be intercepted by a third party with no claim to the property apart from one of convenience (and convenience so defined on the part of the interloping beneficiary to benefit itself, since it would be the courts—an arm of the government—apportioning ownership to the Crown!). Distribution back to the employees, whatever the scheme employed, is strongly preferred over the misappropriation of such funds by the State. This arrangement would be logistically feasible per the contract-holding theory under which, failing a contractual arrangement delineating ownership upon dissolution, equal division should be assumed (including in *Davis*, where the issue was raised as to the due contributions of different classes of employee). Such criticism is especially valid in light of Lord Millett's support for a resulting trust being created to apportion the respective contributions of employees in *Air Jamaica v Charlton* (1999).

Non-charitable Purpose Trusts

Ever since the watershed case of *Re Astor's Settlement Trusts* (1952), the courts have refused to recognize trusts designed to achieve a non-charitable purpose when lacking in human beneficiaries, thereby violating the so-called beneficiary principle established in *Morice v Bishop of Durham* (1804). As articulated by Viscount Simonds on behalf of the Privy Council in *Leahy v Attorney-General of New South Wales* (1960):

> A gift can be made to persons (including a corporation) but it cannot be made to a purpose or to an object: so also a trust may be created for the benefit of persons as *cestuis que trust* but not for a purpose or object unless the purpose or object be charitable. For a purpose or object cannot sue, but, if it be charitable, the Attorney-General can sue to enforce it.[1]

The judgment is sound in that a charitable purpose trust will not be defeated owing to the absence of a human beneficiary, as its worthwhile aims may still be executed by the Attorney-General. Dissimilarly, non-charitable purpose trusts do not perform an intrinsic social good (especially considering that the list of charitable purposes is both very extensive and flexible); the courts should accordingly be reluctant to enforce what may prove—impractical at best (capricious or deleterious at worst)—the will of the settlor. Examples of the sorts of trusts the courts have historically struck down include one aimed at the erection of a monument in dedication of the settlor himself[2] and the development of a new 40-letter alphabet in which the plays of George Bernard Shaw were supposed to be translated.[3] Moreover, the courts' reluctance to enforce these trusts does not extend to trusts designed to benefit, even indirectly, human ben-

---

1 [1959] A.C. 479
2 *Re Endacott* (1960)
3 *Re Shaw* (1957)

eficiaries.[1] Only private purpose trusts with no such discernible beneficiaries will be void.[2]

Nevertheless, there remain outstanding and anomalous exceptions to the rule that private purpose trusts are void. Whilst the following cases occurred before *Re Astor's Settlement Trust*, for the sake of promoting clarity in this area of trust law, their potential precedential value should be clearly terminated, either in ongoing judgments relating to non-charitable trusts, or, even more forcefully, through legislation. The three main areas in which private purpose trusts remain valid include the care of specified animals, the upkeep of monuments or graves and the commission of privately-sponsored masses. Taking them in order, animal welfare was upheld in *Pettingall v Pettingall* (1842), where the testator bequeathed £50 for the ongoing care of his beloved mare. This was followed in *Re Dean* (1889) where a trust was valid in the sum of £750 to support a collection of horses and dogs formerly owned by the testator. *Mussett v Bingle* (1876) recognized that the maintenance of graves was valid grounds for a trust, in which £300 was granted to preserve the gravesite of the former husband of the wife of the testator.[3] This was followed in *Pirbright v Salwey* (1896) and later in *Re Hooper* (1932).

---

1 As stated by Goff J in *Re Denley's Trust Deed* [1969] 1 Ch 384: 'Where, then, the trust, though expressed as a purpose, is directly or indirectly for the benefit of an individual or individuals, it seems to me that it is in general outside the mischief of the beneficiary principle.' This sensible judgment struck a balance in those cases where a private purpose trust may be legitimate so long as there are named beneficiaries or beneficiaries who may be plausibly ascertained. The confusion exists insofar as valid private trusts for the benefit of human beneficiaries may at first blush appear as invalid private purpose trusts, if so worded as to imply their benefit being implemented in regards to a specific purpose or end-result being achieved. In *Re Denley*, the confusion arose because the trust in question sought to create a recreational area for a large number of company employees. It was ultimately held not to be a pure purpose trust because the class of beneficiaries was sufficiently ascertainable to possess the requisite *locus standi* to enforce the trust.
2 *Re Endacott* (1960)
3 This particular anomaly should be abolished subsequent to s.1 of the Parish Councils and Burial Authorities (Miscellaneous Provisions) Act 1970, whereby a private grave may be publicly looked after for a period not to exceed 99 years.

Perhaps most striking is the allowance of trusts promoting prayers said on behalf of a named individual, as was upheld in *Bourne v Keane* (1919). Though the trust in this case was dedicated to pay for facilitating private masses, the comparatively recent case of *Re Hetherington* (1989) held that masses in which the public may participate are considered charitable. Considering the limited role religious services hold in conferring a public benefit, both in terms of those of faith generally and those further subdivided into the category of those who attend the specific church in question (let alone the indemonstrable efficacy of prayer generally as regards promoting a particular beneficial end), the soundness of the court's judgment is dubious. The anachronistic nature of these undertakings is such that the courts should no longer recognize their continuing legitimacy in law, both for reasons of public policy (such as their contestable conception of the Good pursued, such as regards the promotion of particularistic religious ends) and as a means of discouraging any further proliferation of such exceptions in this modern day and age.

The Future of Equity

It is not for us to see what may come beyond the immediacy of the present, and yet we are each inextricably drawn toward speculation in this matter. The law is no stranger to the itch of reformers, who are never contented with the cracks, both visible and otherwise, in the structure of the *status quo*, and equity, traditionally viewed as amongst the most arcane and unchanging disciplines of law, is in fact one whose continuing moral evolution proves more relevant today than ever before amidst a common law straitjacketed by procedure and a concern for form over substance. That is to say that the ongoing importance of equity exists not so much in its adaptation to changing social, economic or cultural conditions (although equity is no doubt sensitive to the demands of shifting norms, as evidenced in its recent attempts to rid itself of the presumption of advancement or in the vigor injected into the domestic constructive trust), but rather in its reinforcement of the moral core necessary for the edifice of law itself to maintain legitimacy and the goodwill of the populace. Unlike ethics, the law is principally concerned with the external administration of society, and toward this end efficacy is the hallmark of its success. Moral duty is a necessarily personal experience, whose diversity of interpretation renders it seemingly hopeless to impose at a societal level. The law rather seeks to establish that lowest common denominator of values which ensures broad compliance amongst all classes of person, regardless of race, sex, faith or wealth. And, it is herein argued that the ultimate value of law is the preservation of justice—the balancing of the competing rights and duties of citizens—which permits the social order and normative flourishing of society at large. Equity is that branch most concerned with its judicious application in the individual case, and its elevation to that of a quasi-moral science, insofar as the unwieldy administrative behemoth that is the law may permit.

As the law is ultimately concerned with procedural efficiency and majoritarian appeasement (in that a law unpopular with the vast majority shall lose its effectiveness and therefore likely be repealed if repeated attempts at implementation fail), its moral development can only occur incrementally. Equity is the solitary tip upon the sword of ethical progress, its influence over the refinement of the remaining content of law straddling the worlds of both social policy and proprietary interest. Nowhere are the crossroads of the *status quo* and future reform more sharply visible; the trust is a device as much for the preservation of inherited privilege as it is a means of ensuring domestic equality between the sexes, proprietary estoppel as concerned with the importance of contractual formality as it is the prevention of an unconscionable outcome. The charge of equity is to morally maturate the law, raising its standards beyond that of our baser natures. Such is acutely evident in the difference between generalized legal and equitable duties. While there is no general positive duty to aid others or act in good faith under the common law, such are paramount features of the duties of a trustee at equity.

Equally, the moral scope of equity is nuanced in a way unknown to the common law in its sensitivity to both public policy *and* idiographic justice. Whereas the latter is a blunt instrument best equipped to deal with the multiplied effects of its precedential value, equity is best able to deal with the specific and substantive facets of a case whose treatment is essential if a unique and just outcome is to be delivered. In this sense, the moral perspective of equity is more advanced, catering to the self-interest of individual litigants through remedies *in personam* (*e.g.,* specific performance and injunctions) rather than the monolithic multitudes, however uninvolved their sheer numbers may prove to the impact of a case (such as where, for instance, the economic impact of adopting a particular ruling is misguidedly adjudged as too costly).[1] Meanwhile, equity is simultaneously able to cater toward collective interests, even when potentially detrimental to individual claimants. This is especially in regard to the validity of trusts whose purpose is capricious (albeit not illegal)—that is, contrary to any semblance of reasonableness or practicability—whereby the will of the settlor may be overridden in the interests of ensuring collective welfare.

In assessing the breadth and import of this inimitable legal discipline, it perhaps behooves us to recount the presciently immortal words of Sir John Trevor MR over three centuries ago:

> Equity is no part of the law, but a moral virtue, which qualifies, moderates and reforms the rigour, hardness and edge of the law, and is a universal truth; it does also assist the law where it is defective and weak in the constitution (which is the life of the law) and de-

---

1 Such was the case in *Marc Rich & Co AG v Bishop Rock Co Ltd and others* (1995), where the imposition of a duty of care upon a marine classification society was not considered 'fair, just and reasonable' despite negligence on its part, owing to the adverse economic ripple effect such duty would have for such organizations owing to the likelihood of their subsequently requiring liability insurance.

fends the law from crafty evasions, delusions, and new subtleties, invented and contrived to evade and delude the common law, whereby such as have undoubted right are made remediless. And thus is the office of equity to protect and support the common law from shifts and contrivances against the justice of the law. Equity, therefore, does not destroy the law, nor create it, but assists it.[1]

Our most fervent hope is that the moral ambition of this nonpareil legal discipline continues to burn brightly throughout this nascent century, ever tempering the edge of the sword of justice. For, just as there can be no law without appeal to our universal conscience, nor may the principle of equity thrive absent the suppleness to judge a man as an individual moral being, unrestrained by the four corners of any statute or contract. This is the essential aspiration of equity, and whilst no contrivance of man is beyond fault, it is toward this venerable purpose that we dedicate ourselves with ceaseless improvement. Let us hope the promise of justness blossoms more fully with each passing generation, ultimately realizing the potential of law as the purest and only necessary guardian of the collective moral spirit of our time.

---

1 *Lord Dudley v Lady Dudley* (1705) Pr. Ch. 241

INDEX

Index of Cases Cited